HER STORIES

HER STORIES

African American Folktales, Fairy Tales, and True Tales

told by

VIRGINIA HAMILTON

illustrated by

LEO & DIANE DILLON

THE BLUE SKY PRESS

An Imprint of Scholastic Inc. • New York

THE BLUE SKY PRESS

Text copyright © 1995 by Virginia Hamilton
Illustrations copyright © 1995 by Leo and Diane Dillon

For information regarding permission, please write to:
Permissions Department,
The Blue Sky Press, an imprint of Scholastic Inc.,
555 Broadway, New York, New York 10012.

The Blue Sky Press is a trademark of Scholastic Inc.

The stories in this book have been gathered from a great number of sources,
and in most cases, many versions exist. The author wishes to thank
the following for permission to use source materials:

Negro Tales from Pine Bluff, Arkansas, and Calvin, Michigan by Richard M. Dorson.
Copyright 1958 © by Richard M. Dorson. Used by permission of Indiana University Press.

Folk Stories of the South by M. A. Jagendorf. Copyright © 1972 by M. A. Jagendorf.
Used by permission of Vanguard Press, a division of Random House, Inc.

"Bat Woman" by Hewitt L. Ballowe. From *The Lawd Sayin' the Same: Negro Folk Tales
of the Creole Country* by Hewitt L. Ballowe. Copyright © 1947 by Hewitt L. Ballowe.
Used by permission of Louisiana State University Press.

"No Stick-Leg," as collected by Bernice Kelly Harris. From *Such As Us: Southern Voices of the Thirties*,
edited by Tom E. Terrill and Jerrold Hirsch. Copyright © 1978 by University of North Carolina Press.
Used by permission of the publisher.

Permission was granted by Mary Lou Thornton to use the text of "Mary Lou Thornton:
My Family" as written by Virginia Hamilton.

"The Mer-Woman Out of the Sea" is a retelling of John Bennett's "The Apothecary and the Mermaid,"
originally published by Rinehart & Company, Inc. in *The Doctor to the Dead*, © 1943, 1946.

Many thanks also to Leanne Seabright, researcher. Her keen eye for detail in the investigation
of source records helped greatly in the uncovering of inspired and unusual material.

Library of Congress Cataloging-in-Publication Data
Hamilton, Virginia.
Her stories: African American Folktales/told by Virginia Hamilton;
illustrated by Leo and Diane Dillon.
p.   cm.
ISBN 0-590-47370-0
ISBN 0-590-56603-2 (Limited Edition)
1.   Afro-American women — Folklore.   I.   Dillon, Leo, ill.
II.   Dillon, Diane, ill.   III.   Title.
GR111.A47H35   1995   398.2'082 — dc20   94-33055   CIP   AC
12 11 10 9   01 02 03 04 05
First printing, October 7, 1995

To our mothers and grandmothers, aunts and great-aunts.

To all the women who stood before us,

telling us about where they came from,

what they saw, did, and imagined.

They let us know they stood for us.

Talking, they combed our hair, rocked us to sleep,

sang to us, told us tales of then and now—

and tomorrow. They worried about us.

They hoped for us and showed us the way.

They cared.

V.H.

To Bon and Louise Jefferson

L. & D.D.

CONTENTS

A NOTE FROM THE AUTHOR   xi

HER ANIMAL TALES

Little Girl and Buh Rabby   3
Buh Rabby Comes By   2

Lena and Big One Tiger   7
Big One Tiger, Dressed Up All Swell   9

Marie and Redfish   11
The Prince, Changed into a Fish   13

Miz Hattie Gets Some Company   15
The Lord's Glove, Transformed   18

HER FAIRY TALES

Catskinella   23

    Skintight and All Shimmery, Too   25

Good Blanche, Bad Rose, and the Talking Eggs   28

    Two Axes, Fighting in Midair   30

Mary Belle and the Mermaid   33

    Down and Way Down, Deep in the Water   35

Mom Bett and the Little Ones A-Glowing   39

    "Little Hers and Hims Tippy-Toed on Cobwebs"   38

HER SUPERNATURAL

Who You!   45

    Each and Every One an Owl   49

Macie and Boo Hag   51

    Boo Hag, in the Night-Riding   53

Lonna and Cat Woman   56

    The Her-Vampire Spells   59

Malindy and Little Devil   61

    They Swung and Swayed Up and Down the Path   64

HER FOLKWAYS AND LEGENDS

Woman and Man Started Even   69

Woman Holds the Keys   73

Luella and the Tame Parrot   75

The Mistress's Bird, Discovered   76

The Mer-Woman Out of the Sea   78

"He Keeps Her *with His Ungodly Things"*   81

Annie Christmas   84

Annie, Dressed Up Like a Fine Lady   87

HER TRUE TALES

Millie Evans: Plantation Times   93

Lettice Boyer: From Way Back   96

Mary Lou Thornton: My Family   101

MORE ABOUT *HER STORIES*   105

USEFUL SOURCES   111

ABOUT THE AUTHOR AND ILLUSTRATORS   113

A NOTE FROM THE AUTHOR

HER STORIES: *African American Folktales, Fairy Tales, and True Tales* brings together narratives about females from the vast treasure store of traditional black folklore. For the first time, African American fairy tales, animal stories, supernatural tales, legends, and true narratives of the female kind are presented in a single volume.

In the past, such tales were gathered by individual collectors and written down in the speaking styles of early storytellers. Therefore, the *soundings* of a tale were often different from story to story. Moreover, collectors had styles of recording stories that were as different as the tellers' ways of telling them.

Some of the stories in this book were recorded in Gullah, a form of English that includes grammar, words, and phrases from African languages. Gullah was first spoken by slaves in the Sea Islands of Georgia, the Carolinas, and Florida. Other tales come from Louisiana and people there who had a combination of Creole ancestries. The language spoken was a Creolized English — that is, English enriched by words and phrases taken from black culture, French, and/or Spanish languages, and by the creation of new words. Still other stories come from wherever early African Americans found themselves. Many of these stories have a familiar- and traditional-sounding black folktale ring to them. A few draw from European and Asian sources.

I have recast these stories for young readers and their older allies. They are composed anew in my own written-down style of telling from the forms in which they were told in the past by other tellers and collectors. I have stayed as close as possible to the style of stories told in a particular region.

Among the African American tales about females are sunny and magical stories, jokey tales, strange tales of foreboding, and frightening ones as well. But there is not a great supply of any of them, as there seems to be of those told about males.

In *Her Stories,* females are portrayed as fairies, mermaids, witches, and animals. In the fairy tale "Catskinella," a young girl's life is transformed when she dresses in a gown made from the skin of a cat. Animals and half-fish creatures share the stage with human females. Supernatural stories, such as "Macie and Boo Hag," accent the frightening and ghostly elements of the black folktale genre.

The story "Annie Christmas" presents a view of legendary folklore. Annie Christmas was said to be a notorious riverboat operator working the Mississippi River around New Orleans. Tales of Annie come to us handed down through black folklore, which accepts her as a woman who once lived. Probably we'll never know for certain if she did live. But it really doesn't matter. Her story is a vivid, true-sounding account that likely has some basis in fact.

Many types of women are portrayed in *Her Stories*. They are various ages and have human shortcomings as well as strengths. They are hard and bright; cold, rough, fearful, mean, and stubborn; fiery, strong, witty, and kind. *Her Stories* also includes true stories about real African American women who we know actually lived.

In the centuries of the Plantation Era, the black slave woman was the keeper of households. She was a laborer without pay for any work, from dayclean to daylean — sunup to sundown. When the owner's work was done, she went home to her cabin and helped take care of her own family. At supper, she might think of a riddle to amuse her children. And after, she would whisper plans and dreams with her husband.

Often, the late night was her time alone. Again and again, she let her tired mind fly free to remember good times. And when there weren't any, she made up what such times would be like. She imagined all kinds of things — birds and other animals talking to her in the woods or fields. She worried about the silent dark pressing against the cabin windows. Some said there were ghosts and witches, fairies and magic in that great, lonesome night.

So it was she made up *her* stories, some out of her own imagination and others she'd heard told by both men and women. These last she would alter to fit her experience. Later in the dayclean, she passed tales along to her own children and those in her care.

That is how I imagine some of *Her Stories,* household tales, first came to be. Such stories have continued to be devised and told. For stories of the female kind have a wide, creative range. They are difficult to categorize and often fit more than one type. Having grown out of the generational folkways of African Americans, they represent a body of traditional lore that is uniquely American.

Her Stories are meant for you to enjoy. Read them to yourselves, or read them out loud. By all means, share them with one another.

VIRGINIA HAMILTON, 1995

HER ANIMAL TALES

THE CLOSE RELATIONSHIP between humans and animals is an important subject in African American folktales. In "Her Animal Tales," deceptions, hoaxes, tricks, conjure, and creation are played out with human and animal participants on a broad, folkloric stage.

Young females and women take on fairly traditional roles in these tales: A little girl is home alone, watching the home place for her mother until her father returns; an older woman seeks companionship; a young woman plans to marry a perfect man; and a maiden, courted by a prince, is undone by magic.

For centuries, females in association with animals have been the subject of folktales throughout the world, as can be seen in the internationally popular "Beauty and the Beast" story. African American tales carry on the tradition in this variety of female-and-animal tales.

LITTLE GIRL AND BUH RABBY

LITTLE GIRL was always home. Her mama had her go down, pick some peas in the garden. "Now I must go to market, take my vegetables every day," Mama told her. "Today, you mind the house and garden. Couple days from now, you can come along."

"I'll mind everything, I will," says Little Girl. But soon as Mama was gone, Buh Rabby comes by. Big, stand-up ears, white puff tail.

Says the rabbit, "Little Girl, I see you are picking peas."

"I sure am," says Little Girl. "Mama told me to."

"I saw your mama going out, and she greeted me," said Buh Rabby. "Says to me, 'Tell Little Girl to let you in for some peas.' "

"All right, if Mama said so," Little Girl said. She opened the gate and let Buh Rabby in.

Buh Rabby ate a whole row of sweet, tender peas in a minute. Him, stand-up ears, tail, big ole feet. Says, "Let me out now."

So she did.

Mama came home from market, asked Little Girl how she was doing.

"I let Buh Rabby in like you told him to tell me to," Little Girl said to her mama.

"Well, I never saw him to tell, and I never said anything to that pesty Buh Rabby," her mama told her. "If he comes back tomorrow, you let him in the garden, but don't let him out. When your daddy comes home, he'll help you take care of Buh Rabby."

Next day, Buh Rabby hopped on over. "Hey, there, Little Girl," he said, "I come for to visit the garden."

Little Girl stayed quiet, but she opened the gate, and Buh Rabby hopped inside. White puff tail, big feet, flippity-flop he goes.

Little Girl locked the gate behind Buh Rabby. Puff tail, up and down the sweet-pea row, ears just waving.

Buh Rabby stayed all day. Then, way late, he dragged his full-belly self to the gate. It was almost time for Little Girl's daddy to come home from his labor, too. But that rabbit didn't know a thing.

Buh Rabby called Little Girl, hollered at her: "Girl! Turn me loose now. I am all finished here."

Little Girl told him, "I am busy, Buh Rabby. I hasn't no time right now to turn you loose."

So Buh Rabby sat down to wait. He didn't like waiting, but what was he going to do? After a while, he says, real polite, "Little Girl, I must leave right now. Let me out. Please."

She tells him, "Buh Rabby, can't you see I am fixing these sweet peas for my mama? I can't be bothered with you!"

Little Girl's daddy came home right then. He saw what was in the garden besides Little Girl. Buh Rabby, that's what. All ears, puff tail, and big feet.

"What are you doing in there?" asked the daddy.

Buh Rabby tells him, "Little Girl let me in here, sir."

"Commere, I got something for you better than them pea pods," Daddy told Buh Rabby.

Buh Rabby hopped to the gate, flippity-flop. Little Girl and her daddy grabbed him by the ears. They stuffed him in a gunnysack and hung him in the wild honey locust. Up and down its trunk and branches, that tree had thorns as long as a man's finger.

"Ole Buh Rabby is high-strung and prickled!" Little Girl told her mama. Her daddy went away in the woods to cut some switches; going to smart Buh Rabby for sure.

But Wolf came along, heard Buh Rabby coughing in the gunnysack. Said, "That you, Rabby? What you doing in there?"

"Oh," said Buh Rabby, thinking fast. "I'm on my way to Heaven for Little Girl. You want to come along?"

"Yes, indeed!" said the wolf.

"Then open my sack and come on in," Buh Rabby told him.

So big ole Wolf did it, he jumped in. Buh Rabby jumped out, tied the wolf in the gunnysack. "Hey!" hollered Wolf. But Buh Rabby was gone, even before he started, fast as he could get.

Little Girl and her daddy came back. She gave the sack a once-over, said, "You're no rabbit in there. Wolf, what you doing?"

"I'm a-go to Heaven for you, Little Girl, like Buh Rabby say I do if I go in here."

Little Girl giggled, and her daddy smiled. "Now I'm a-going to finish this," Daddy said. "And it won't be Heaven you will get." With that, he switched Wolf's hide about ten-sting times.

"Ow-ow-ow!" Wolf hollered.

Daddy said, "When you see a gunnysack again, Wolf, you better take care!"

Little Girl told Wolf, "And you make sure Buh Rabby won't hide a trick in it, too!"

Anybody see that Little Girl at the market, tell her:

I go around the bend.

I see a fence to mend.

On it is hung my story end.

COMMENT: This comical tale has two familiar motifs: the false message (Rabby says Mama said to let him in the garden) and substitution of one for another (Wolf for Rabbit). The false-message tale has many variants, which increases its value as a true folktale. Such tales are told, added to, repeated, and changed again and again.

In some versions, the child is called Little Daughter. The name Buh Rabby is an old variation of Bruh or Brer (Brother) Rabbit. The daughter and her helpers (Mama and Daddy) prevail over the rabbit. Buh Rabby is undone by Little Girl and her daddy. Buh Rabby, in turn, outsmarts Wolf and frees himself at last.

The tricky Buh Rabby usually wins over other animals. In Plantation Era times, the slaves identified with the small, defenseless rabbit, who nevertheless could get in and out of just about any difficulty.

The rhyme is a typical ending to such folktales.

LENA AND BIG ONE TIGER

THERE WAS this glory-looking young girl in the time when animals talked. She was Lena, beauty. And she was always saying, "I'll never marry any man who is marked wounded." She meant any man scarred or clawed. Said it all the time.

And then there was that animal, called Big One Tiger. He heard Lena talking from a way off. He thought she was pretty, and he decided to turn himself into a young man. He dressed himself up all swell, and he drove to Lena's house in a real fine buggy.

Lena saw that buggy with a sable horse. She came out to look at the young man buggy riding. She called to her mama, said, "Mama, come on here and see." When her mama come on there, Lena says to her, says, "Right there is the young gentleman I will marry."

"I agree," says Lena's mama. "He certainly is a good-looking man."

Well, Big One Tiger did marry Lena, and he carried her off right then in his handsome buggy, he did. They went way down in the deep swamp where Big One Tiger lived. He put Lena there. "You stay still here," he told her, "until I come back."

Well, Big One left her there with not a thing to eat in this whole world. He left her there with just one fly to mind her, too. And Big One told the fly, "If anybody bothers my Lena, well, you must come to me and tell me."

The fly buzzed right back, "Wwwwilll! Wwwwilll!"

Lena stayed in that swamp for three whole days and nights. She had nothing on her tongue down to her stomach the whole time. There was this ugly, dried-up carcass and one bone left there by Big One Tiger. And that's all she had to look on.

Now this is true — there was an old man who knew Lena's family well. One day, he went out hunting, and the tracks led him to the swamp. He heard hollering. To his great shock, he found Lena there, looking half dead and whole scared. She told the old man, Jacob, "I married this fellow, and he brought me here — don't know why."

Old Jacob told her, "I saw his tracks and yours. He may stand upright, but he's not a man! He's a tiger!"

Lena nearly fainted. She didn't know what to do. Meantime, the fly went to tell Big One that there was someone with Lena.

Big One Tiger came flying back, yelling, "Whoga, whoga, whogalor, da humbarnorta, sundundilly?"

Old Jacob and Lena couldn't make head nor tail of it. And Big One came close, looking like a man, he did, with tiger eyes. He was trying to make Lena lose her faith. He was standing there over Jacob, trying to make him tremble.

But Jacob had the answer, said, "Coo me sormber norty sundundilly indelarun."

And Big One Tiger-Man runs a spear through his own side and says the same thing again. This time, both Lena and Jacob answer him, same way, "Coo me sormber norty sundundilly indelarun."

Then Big One Tiger says, "Well, Lena, you can follow old Jacob out of here. I won't hurt you. I just married you to let you know a woman can't be more than a man. Because you said you wouldn't marry a young man who was marked wounded, I tricked you to show how you didn't know everything." Right away, Big One shifted to four feet and ran off, looking like a tiger.

"Whew!" Lena said. "Glad that's over. He sure fooled me!"

She and Jacob hurried out of there, and never came back.

♀♀♀♀♀

COMMENT: A hundred years ago in the 1890s, this story was told by a woman from the Sea Islands. It is a uniquely peculiar tale belonging to the Plantation Era. In the long-ago past of African Americans, the supreme position of women in their homes in parts of Africa was well established. The mother was the sole guardian of the children. She was also the property holder. She gave the family its name, which was passed on. At one time, this tale might have been told by a man, as a masculine protest against this matriarchal order. Generations later, the woman storyteller found it amusing as well.

The strange words Big One Tiger presents, "Whoga, whoga . . . ," may be nonsense syllables. In any case, the original collector could find no translation. Perhaps they're meant to scare Jacob and Lena with their mysterious sound. Jacob's comeback, "Coo me sormber . . . ," is also a mystery, and sounds humorous.

This is a somewhat rare type of animal shape-shifter story. It draws upon the familiar tale of animal and human in combination yet at odds.

MARIE AND REDFISH

THE YOUNG GIRL, Marie, was courted by a prince. "You're too young for courting," her father told her.

"But I care for him," Marie said.

"I don't want him coming around here," said her father.

He remembered a wizard who lived in the woods. He went to him, saying, "You, Wizard, make the prince leave my child, Marie, alone. I don't want them to marry."

Well, Marie was in love, and one good day, she and her prince were seated by the river. The tiny wizard came near them. He pointed his crooked staff at the prince. Behold! The young man was changed into a fish. The fish jumped high, and into the river, where it disappeared from sight.

Her father was certain that Marie would think the prince had run away, and that she would soon forget about him. The young man was now a fish, after all — this was her father's happy thought. So he and his wife no longer kept a careful watch on their daughter, Marie.

But each day, Marie went to the river and remembered her love. She was so sad, sitting on the riverbank. And one day, she sang:

"Caliwa wa, caliwa co.

Waco, Mother says yes (Maman dit oui).

Waco, Father says no (Papa dit non).

Caliwa wa, caliwa co."

No sooner had she sung than the river seemed to split open. Suddenly, a beautiful red fish wearing a gold crown showed itself. The waters fell together around it as it swam near Marie. Redfish had fruit and sweets for Marie to eat. He placed them at her feet.

So it was that Marie's father noticed that each day she would go to the river. He watched, saw what she did. And one day, he followed her. He brought his gun along. Marie sang, *"Caliwa wa, caliwa co,"* and Redfish surfaced, wearing his crown of gold.

There was Marie's father with his gun. "Boo-loo!" once. "Boo-loo!" twice. He shot the red fish and took it home for his supper.

"Daughter, cook this fish," he told Marie. "I'm sure it will make a tasty dinner for us."

Marie had to do it. She had to prepare Redfish for cooking. But when she went to scale him, Redfish sang mournfully:

"Cut me, oh, if you must, wa, wa.

Scrape me, oh, if you have to, wa, wa.

Mix the crumbs, salt them, wa, wa."

Marie cooked the fish. And when it was done, she served it to her

father. She sat down. Inside, she was crying her heart out for her dear prince, Redfish.

Marie's father ate and ate of fish. He ate and ate, stuffing himself. Until — *pla-oomp*! his big belly burst open. Lo! And many little fishes fell out. They slid themselves, squiggling, to the river.

After dinner, Marie left the house. She went to the riverbank, of course, to sit awhile just where the scales of her loving Redfish were scattered. Weeping hard, her tears made the earth open before her. She fell into the hole.

Down, deep down under, Marie met her Redfish. Right before her eyes, he changed into a prince again, wearing a gold crown.

When her mother came looking for Marie, she found only a lock of her daughter's hair. That was all that was left. A long, dark curl, spread out on the earth.

COMMENT: Also considered a fairy tale, this sad story is called "Le Poisson d'Or," or "The Golden Fish" in French, and is now told by the French Creole community of Louisiana.

More than a century ago, the lock of Marie's hair left hanging out of the earth was thought a comical ending to an otherwise pathetic love story. One curious, yet engaging, part of this tale is the song the daughter sings to her fish and the one he sings back to her while being cut and salted.

"Waco," "caliwa wa," and "wa wa" are not translated in the story. These insistent refrain soundings are used by Creole singers today. They give further expressive emphasis to the song chants.

The structure of this folktale is similar to the French *chantefable* — or cante fable — a prose narrative with verse. It is a common structure in southern black folktales.

MIZ HATTIE GETS SOME COMPANY

ONCE UPON TIME, when dogs barked rhyme, there was Miz Hattie. Miz Hattie lived all alone in the piney woods. It was all right for her in the spring when trees bloomed and flowers covered the ground. Then, she'd sit on her porch, rocking in her rocking chair. Feeling at peace with herself, she'd murmur, "The whole bright world is here for me to look on."

Life was good to her in summer when the sunshine warmed the pines. It was even better in the fall when all was ripe. Hattie was busy then getting her corn and taters and pumpkins in, and her wood for the cold weather.

But when winter came with heavy snows, the pine trees rocked, and the wind howled so. "Woo-hooo! Woo-hooo!" went the wind, hauling snow all around the house and down the chimney.

It made Hattie feel low and very down in her mind. "Wish I had me somebody close," she whispered. "Maybe a child, or a sister. I'm about as lonesome as a biscuit without some gravy."

Miz Hattie had other bothers, too. Hawks and minks and foxes stole her chickens. Rats and mice gnawed her corn and taters. "The varmints are about starving me out of my house and home," she complained to the woods.

She was afraid of the rats and mice. Especially the mice. They were smart enough to know. They'd watch her from their holes in the cabin logs, and then they'd scoot out and run right across her feet. She hollered, "Mercy me!" and gathered her skirts up.

Then the mice would fairly snicker at her. Oh, yes! They tripped her and jumped out at her. They hid in the cornmeal bag and leaped out when she stuck her hand in.

One cold night, bad went to worse with a swirl of sparks in the fireplace. A whole squeak of mice started up playing hide-and-seek in the sugar bowl and tag around the bread box. They took flying leaps and landed on the bedcovers. They did mouse springs right on top of poor Miz Hattie's head.

Hattie gave a yell like nothing the mice had heard before. Loud as the wind, it was — *"Oh, mercy sakes! Lord, help me!"* She flung her arms and kicked the creatures tangled in her quilt — clear to the floor.

The quilt folded down, and mice flew every which way, hitting the walls and skidding on their backs into their holes. They sat there trembling, afraid to make even a squeak. They'd never seen Miz Hattie so mad.

Oh, it was a powerful cold night, too. Suddenly, there came a giant crunching on the snow. Monstrous steps came a-scrunching and sounding as deep as a dungeon.

The steps halted at Miz Hattie's door. A hammer knock sounded like the rush-roar of a blizzard. It caused Miz Hattie's teeth to shake in her gums. "Land-a-mercy, what's going to happen to me?" she moaned. Yet she never lost her manners. She managed to call out in a high voice, "Come in, whoever it be, and Heaven help me!"

The door flew open. Right there stood the Lord himself, come all the way down to help Miz Hattie.

She found herself out of bed and sitting on her stool. She knew who it was and sat, bowed down for a moment, awed and respectful. She couldn't help staring. Seemed he was inside and outside at once. She could see the moon and stars through his head and shoulders.

He didn't say a word to her at first. He pulled off one of his gloves and threw it on the floor. And that glove, lo! It started to squirm and wiggle, yes, it did! Hattie couldn't believe her eyes. "Lord, is your glove a-moving there?" she asked.

Gently, he told her, "I believe it be, Miz Hattie."

"Whatever *you* say has to be," she answered.

Sure enough, she saw the thumb of the glove turn into a tail. And the fingers turned into four legs. The gauntlet became a head. In no time, the glove had changed into a creature that stretched itself and worked its claws. It sniffed at the mouse tracks.

By-and-by, the creature sprang at one of the bad little skeezicks that poked its head too far out of its hole. Bless it be, the creature caught the mouse. With a fatal bite, it laid the mouse at Miz Hattie's feet. Showing her what it could do for her.

Miz Hattie took up the creature, that cat, what it was. Held it in her arms and stroked it and nuzzled it some. The cat was so pleased, it hunched down in her lap and made a warm, purring sound deep inside itself. Yes, and cats have been purring ever since. This first cat made the noise so much that Miz Hattie started calling it Purralee.

Well, Miz Hattie had forgot all about the Lord standing there, she was so happy. And when she remembered to thank him, she looked up only to

find the door closed. There was nobody there. She thought she'd dreamed the whole thing.

She did not! Because even right now, when cats are angry, they look like fingers clinched up tight to the hand. And until can't can, they wiggle-waggle their tails, just like a daddy's thumb warning to say, "Un-uh! Don't do that!" to the child.

After then, every time Miz Hattie hollered, "Purralee, Purralee," the cat came running to her and rubbed itself against her legs.

And that's how the cat came to be. You must always watch out for them, for they're made of Jesus' glove. And it's plain unlucky to harm them. Still, cats came here well after other creatures, and so they should behave themselves. But they never do. They think cream and meat were made for them, and the softest cushion, too, like Miz Hattie's lap.

But she was happy now, dear Miz Hattie was. She had some company at last. So be it, bow bended, don't you know. My story's ended.

COMMENT: A longish tale, but a sweet one! It was first told by elderly black tellers in southwestern Virginia and written down in the colloquial speech of the Plantation Era, generations before the Civil War. It is a *pour-quoi* — or why — story and a creation story, in which the Lord created the cat for Miz Hattie because she was so lonely. We don't know if it was a man or a woman who first told this story. In any case, "Miz Hattie Gets Some Company" has a gentle, wise humor that seems fitting in a story about an elderly black woman alone.

The rhyming phrases at the story's beginning and end are common to many Plantation Era African American folktales.

HER FAIRY TALES

FAIRY TALES are folktales not necessarily about fairies. They are about the unusual, the different, and the fantastical, and they give accounts of magical and enchanting events.

A fairy tale might have a struggle between good and bad. There can be a journey, a quest, a test, or a task to perform. For the good woman or child, the outcome is success and happiness.

However, these African American fairy tales have several subtle characters that are not revealed as entirely good or bad. And sometimes, the happy endings are elusive. The black seafaring people who told the tale of "Mary Belle and the Mermaid," for example, knew that bad could follow good. Either way, we are at once there in these stories, as the narration unfolds a time and a place of enchantment.

CATSKINELLA

UPON TIME, there was Ella. Oh, she had a beautiful face! Ella's father wanted her to marry a woodsman. But Ella didn't take to him. "Tell him he must first give me a looking-glass mirror that can talk." Smiling, she knew that would take time!

Her father told the young woodsman what Ella had said. And one day, the woodsman came back with a talking mirror. He did! Mirror said to the father, "See me? I see you!" Talking as big as it pleased.

Ella didn't know what she would do; she didn't want to marry just yet. So she found her godmother, Mattie, and said, "Oh, Mother Mattie, the woodsman will marry me if I don't watch out."

"Tell your daddy to go kill a cat," said Mother Mattie. "He's to take its hide and have a dress made out of it for you. Have him tell the woodsman to give you a ring for the engagement."

So Ella told her father, and he did as Mother Mattie had said. And soon, he got Ella a black catskin dress for the wedding. She put it on. It was skintight and all shimmery, too. She was dressed up — Catskinella. And the woodsman gave a ring over to her father. And Ella's father gave it to her.

Now Catskinella was in trouble. She still didn't want to be a bride. What to do? She didn't know, so she went back to her godmother.

Mother Mattie told her, "You get ready day after tomorry to marry the woodsman. Make his dressing room upstairs, and you dress downstairs. Have the looking-glass mirror right there in your dressing room to talk to."

Catskinella pretended to get dressed up to wed, smoothing that catskin dress just so. She locked the downstairs room strong, with her and the looking glass in it. Then she climbed out the window.

Next hour, her father hollered down, "Are you ready yet, Daughter?"

"Not quite ready yet!" the mirror hollered back.

Father called down again and then again. The woodsman called down, too. But each time, the looking glass hollered back, "Not quite ready yet!"

Finally, Ella's father and the woodsman broke down the door. The father saw the looking glass looking at him. He smashed it.

But Catskinella had run away, fast as she could go.

When she saw the king's castle, she went there for safety. She still had her beautiful face. The king's son saw her face, nothing else — not that scary, skintight catskin. He fell way deep in love with her, too. Everybody else — King, Queen — just stared at that catskin.

The son found Catskinella work minding the chickens. So she stayed back there in a little cabin all her own. And the prince snuck back there every day, lovesick him! He spied on Catskinella when she thought she was all alone.

And see! She shook her catskin gown. It shimmered. And there came

these changes — all so pretty dresses, all colors, like the sunlight and moonlight mixed. And Catskinella looked like a beautiful girl, and not just in her face.

The prince went to bed, just sick with love. He asked the queen for good cake made by a pretty hand, to comfort him. King commanded the maidens of the kingdom to each make a cake. The best cake-maker would marry the ailing prince.

All of the maidens baked cakes, but none suited the prince's taste. He turned away, saying, "How about asking pretty Ella to make me one?"

"You mean, that girl with the catskin?" asks the queen.

"She's got the most beautiful face I ever saw," says the sick prince. Couldn't see nothing else; he was just love-blind.

So someone told Catskinella, "The prince wants you to make him a cake."

Ella answered, "Why should I? Oh, well, I will. He found me a place to work and a cabin to live in."

Ella made the cake and dropped her ring in the batter. Queen put it with the rest of the cakes, but Ella's was the one the prince took a bite of. He didn't know whose cake it was. He took another bite, and he bit on that ring. He took it up, saw what it was. Smiled, kissed the ring, put it under his pillow. "I'll find out whose finger fits this ring," he said, and went to sleep.

So the next day, the king summoned all the young girls there. Each maiden tried the ring, but none could get it on a finger.

The prince called for Catskinella. "Bring her to me, quick!"

"What do you want her for?" Queen wanted to know. But he called for her, anyway.

The servant brought her in. Ella tried on the ring. "That was easy!" she said. "The ring belongs to me."

Ella shivered once, twice. She shook her catskin gown. Oh, so! She glittered and glimmered in a dress of precious diamonds. They all had to cover their eyes. Did too! Then they saw she was beautiful, in a fine gold-and-silver dress fit for a princess. Just swell, down to the little silk slippers she was wearing. All that catskin vanished off her.

"Now she is exactly the one, and I knew she was," said the prince. "Will you marry me, Ella?"

"Of course I'll marry you!" Catskinella said.

"Thank you, Ella," he said back.

So they got married and lived happily. But the looking-glass mirror never talked out of turn again. It was all broken up over everything!

COMMENT: This is a delightful version of the ageless Cinderella story. A magic catskin is just what it sounds like. Other variants call it a jackskin, which could be a donkey skin or the skin of a jackrabbit. Neither changes the story.

Probably, the Cinderella motif was mixed in with that of the cat as woman/witch. African American tellers often utilized cats in their stories, and other animals that were common where they lived. Witches became cats and vice versa. They shed their skins and flew away.

The mirror is a folk motif borrowed from older fairy tales — "Mirror, mirror, on the wall . . ." In this tale, it "reflects" Catskinella's wishes. The transformation motif in the story is common to fairy tales. This classic tale has been altered or added to by numbers of communities around the world.

GOOD BLANCHE, BAD ROSE, AND THE TALKING EGGS

THE TWO DAUGHTERS were good Blanche and bad Rose. Their mama loved bad Rose best because Rose was her spitting image. Mama made good Blanche do all the housework, while bad Rose did nothing but rock back and forth in her rocking chair.

One day, Mama sent Blanche out with a bucket to get her cold, fresh water. Blanche did as she was told. At the well, she saw an old woman. The woman said, "My little one, little one, give me some water. I am so thirsty."

"Yes, Auntie," said Blanche, kindly. "Here is plenty of fresh water for you." She filled the bucket and gave some water to the old woman.

"Ah," sighed the woman, after she drank two cupfuls. "Thank you, my little one, little one. You are such a good girl, bless your heart."

Then Blanche refilled the bucket and carried the heavy load all the way home without spilling any of the fresh water.

Not long after this, the mother acted so mean toward her that Blanche ran away, deep into the woods. Hidden in the trees, she went here and there, crying and wringing her hands. She was all alone and afraid to go home. She didn't know what to do.

Suddenly, she saw the old woman walking in front of her.

"Little one, little one, why are you crying?" the old woman asked Blanche. "What hurts you?"

"Oh, Auntie," Blanche said. "My mama hit me. I'm too afraid to go home."

"Well, come with me, then," said the old woman. "I will give you some supper and a bed to sleep in. But you mustn't laugh at what you will see."

She and Blanche walked hand in hand, on through the woods. Thorny bushes opened before them and then closed behind them. Farther along, Blanche saw two axes fighting in midair.

That's very strange, she thought, but she said nothing.

As she and the old woman walked on, Blanche saw two arms without bodies, with fists, punching. Next, she saw two heads bumping each other.

Blanche was shocked and confused, but she kept quiet — for they had reached the woman's cabin. "Make a fire, then, little one, little one," said the woman. "We'll cook our supper."

The old woman sat down by the fire and took off her head. She placed it on her knees and combed her hair.

How very weird! thought Blanche. This must be a magic place. But she didn't say a word about it.

The old woman put her head back on. She gave Blanche a large bone to put on the fire for their supper. Blanche carefully put the bone in a pot over the fire. At once, the pot was full of good meat to eat. Next, the woman gave Blanche one grain of rice to pound. Soon, the table was full of rice.

After they ate supper, the old woman said, "Little one, little one, scratch my back."

Blanche did as she was told and cut her hand to bleeding. The woman's back was made of broken glass. And when she saw Blanche's hand covered in blood, the old woman blew on it. The hand healed.

Blanche had a good night's sleep. At daybreak, the old woman told her, "Go home now, little one, little one. You are such a good girl, I will give you a present of my talking eggs. In the chicken house, take all the eggs that say, 'Take me.' Leave the ones that say, 'Don't take me.' And when you are on the way home, throw the eggs behind you to break them."

Blanche did as she was told and broke the eggs behind her as she went. Diamonds came out of the eggs. Then gold came, and a beautiful carriage full of fine dresses.

When Blanche got home, she filled the house with riches. Her mama was very glad to see her.

The next day, Mama said to Rose: "Go to the woods, meet the old woman. You must have finer dresses than Blanche."

Rose went to the woods, and all happened as had happened to Blanche. But when Rose saw the axes, the arms, and the heads fighting, she laughed. When the old woman took her head off and set it down on her knees, Rose had to hold her sides, she laughed so hard. And she made fun of everything she saw.

The following day, the old woman said to Rose, "I can't send you home with nothing, Rose, even though you are not so good. Go to the chicken house. Take only the eggs that say, 'Take me.' "

Rose went to the chicken house. Some of the eggs began shouting: "Take me!" Others yelled, "Don't take me!" over and over.

"So you all say," Rose said, "but you don't fool me. I'm taking you who say, 'Don't take me.' "

As she walked away, Rose broke eggs. Out of them came a huge lot of snakes, toads, and frogs, which ran after her. Whips came, and they whipped Rose. She ran, hollering for her mother. "Mama, Mama, help me!" she cried. At home, she was too frightened and tired out to speak.

Mama saw the ground beasts and the whips. She was furious. "Get out of here, Rose, and take those awful things with you. Go live in the woods." She sent Rose away like a dog.

And Rose went, taking her troubles with her.

COMMENT: This tale was collected in the Louisiana Creole colloquial speech. Similar stories are widely known in Europe and the United States. One version was printed in the *Journal of American Folk-Lore* in the late 1800s and titled "The Talking Eggs."

The earliest version likely originated from India, centuries before it was first written down. It made its way to Africa and Europe and, with variations, around the world. As people travel, so their stories travel with them.

MARY BELLE AND THE MERMAID

MARY BELLE was the only daughter. Her mother and father treated her well. Yes, and they all lived on life's pleasant shore. But what happened? The mother got ill, and she died. And it was not long before the father married again. The woman he married had two daughters, name of Bethla and Sadie.

The girls treated Mary Belle, oh, like she didn't belong to anybody. Yes, and they treated her like she wasn't even a speck of dirt. Mary Belle felt so bad all the time, she'd run off to the river. She would just stand on the bank and cry.

One day, there came this thing out of the water. It rose up way high on what looked like its tail.

"What in the world are you?" asked Mary Belle.

"I'm the mermaid what lives in this water," came the answer. "Don't you see my tail?"

"I see you got no legs, and that tail," Mary Belle told her.

"But why do you cry, Mary Belle?" asked the mermaid.

"Well, my good mother died," said Mary Belle. "Then, my own father married a woman who has two daughters, Bethla and Sadie. They keep the meat back from me, they feed me nothing, and they treat me like a stepchild."

"I don't like the sound of that. Come with me," said the mermaid.

Mary Belle went with her. Down and way down, deep in the water. It was real pretty down there, full of fishes and caves and wavery light. The mermaid gave Mary Belle something cool to drink, and lots of food to eat.

Afterward, Mary Belle went on back home. All of them, her father, his wife, and her daughters, were having their supper. They wouldn't give Mary Belle some, either. So mean.

The next day, she went down to the river. Didn't know what came over her, but she had to sing. This is what she sang:

"Down, down, to the deep and shady,

   Pretty mer-maidy, take me down!"

All got still. Then there was a darkening in the river. Next thing, there came the mermaid. She splashed up on her tail, all shimmery silver-blue and gold. She slid on her belly in the waves and lifted her tail over her head like a fan. She came on over, took Mary Belle down. She gave Mary Belle lots of goodies to eat and some sugar, and cream to drink. After a while, she brought Mary Belle up again.

Mary Belle went on home. She just couldn't keep still about it this time. So she told her father and her stepmother.

"I went with a mermaid way in the river. I wouldn't lie to you," Mary Belle told them.

The next day when the sun was going up the sky, all of them went down to the river. So this time, her father sang:

"Mary Belle's been down.
Pretty mer-maidy, take me dow-ow-n."

"That's not the way to do it," says Bethla. "Here, let me sing."
She sang:

"Mary Belle's been, Daddy wants to go.
Pretty mer-maidy, take me dow-ow-n."

They waited a minute. Nothing darkened in the river. Nothing rose up. The youngest, Sadie, said, "Let me do it, let me sing." Sang:

"Mary Belle's been, Daddy can't, Bethla wants to go.
Down, down, to the deep and shady.
Pretty mer-maidy, take me dow-ow-n."

Suddenly, there was a way darkening in the middle of the river. The mermaid came up. It was something about the youngest's voice. Mermaid slid on her belly and came to them on a wave. Her tail was up over her head. It was all sparkly wet and golden. She wiggled it and beckoned them to come to her.

The father, he had a gun. He took it out and shot the poor mermaid through her tail. She shrieked. He shot her again. Now there was bright green foam all around her. She sank way down under and was gone, gone.

Mary Belle never dreamed her father would do what he did. She went away, weeping. Came back the next day. Sang for the mermaid, sang:

"Pretty mer-maidy, it's me, Mary Belle.
Take me down and dow-ow-n."

But the pretty mermaid never came, never rose up. Told you she was gone, gone. Mary Belle didn't know it for certain. And when she did know at last, she walked out into the river. Waded out in the water until it most covered her. And Mary Belle disappeared under the rippling waves.

Gone was she, like the mermaid and like her mother. Gone, gone. All, way gone. True.

Step on a tin, the tin bends. This is how my story ends.

COMMENT: In earlier times, it was reported that African American tales about mermaids were rare. Yet contemporary collectors have uncovered a number of such stories. This one, with its song and sad ending, is a *chante-fable* (cante fable) from South Carolina, dating back to the early 1900s. It was published in 1923 by the American Folk-Lore Society. The storyteller was Ada Bryan, who wrote it down for the folk collector.

There are several mermaid tales that originated in the black and mixed-race communities of the Cape Verde Islands off the African coast. Black Portuguese immigrants brought them to North America and eventually translated them into their new language, English. The Portuguese seafaring families traveled the east coast of the United States. "Mary Belle and the Mermaid" may well have a Portuguese connection.

MOM BETT AND THE
LITTLE ONES A-GLOWING

MOM BETT and her son, Jody, lived in a house at the edge of the fields where the woods began. The garden was shaded by a high, old tree. Mom Bett often said the tree had taken a leap out of the woods right into her heart. Jody said Mom Bett loved the tree more than him. She laughed and teased back: "I love you both the same!"

Every 'fore dayclean, Mom Bett was there to see first light fall over the tree. On Friday, seated on her back porch, she waited for the day to gather in the leaves. Friday was the day when Mom Bett and all the other folks on down the lane kept out of the fields. Folks said Friday work was bad luck, too.

"Stay at home, though, and something good may happen," Mom Bett told Jody. Every Friday, Jody would say, "I'm waiting for something good!" Jody was a kindly young fellow, for true.

Just before dawn this Friday, Mom Bett sat, a cup of tea next to her on the top back step. Her garden of hollyhocks, zinnias, snapdragons, tomatoes, pole beans, and cabbages was in shadow. Then the gentlest 'fore-dawn came in, first in the corners, then shining on the flowers. Dawn light gleamed all over the tree. Yet, it was different, somehow. It was twinkly, like starlight. Next, it was light bursting, like Mom Bett had never seen. It made her catch her breath and sit like a statue. The whole tree lit up like a Christmas tree. Streaking light breathed itself in with a gentle sigh. It poured from the top of the sky to stream down the tree trunk, spreading along every branch.

Floating down with it came these perfect little ones. There were glowing little girl-ones. And little boy shapes. Just the happiest, little delicate ones! They rode light streams down and sprang on the blades of grass. They lounged on the zinnias; two boy-thems lifted dewdrops and tossed them to each other. All-thems danced on the leaves. They fluttered and swayed, glowing like fireflies. Not one of them taller than two inches!

"Little hers and hims tippy-toed on cobwebs," Mom Bett told Jody, later. "Tiny sister- and brother-ones made cobweb swings on the branches. Oh, what a show they gave!"

"Oooh, can I see them little ones? I'll get up with you next Friday morning," Jody promised. And he did, too.

Next Friday came, and Mom Bett and Jody sat as still as stumps just 'fore day. The light gathered, streamed from the blue heaven. And one perfect, floating fairy-her came down out of the tree on a light glow. She flitted before them long enough to smile at them, to swing on the cobwebs an instant. And as the sun rose, she tippy-toed up the tree from one leaf to the next, up into the heavenly light. She vanished, as if she never was. Was she, ever — a good-luck gift of Friday? Hushed, sitting close there, Mom Bett and Jody talked about it for a long time. That's all.

COMMENT: Tales of fairies are few and mostly fragmentary in black folk-lore. This tale by the author is based on sparse evidence. The African American spirit world is one usually to be feared, and it deals mainly with witches, devils, boo hags, and ghosts.

Friday is ominous in African American folklore. "He who laughs on Friday will cry by Sunday," so the saying goes. *Dayclean* is a Gullah word meaning "dawn" or "just before." The late part of the day is known as *daylean* — the sun is "leaning" toward the west.

HER SUPERNATURAL

THE SUPERNATURAL cannot be explained by the laws of nature. It remains forever on the outside, above and beyond what is normal. American folk literature in general is rich with tales of the supernatural.

African American tales abound with weird, mystical, and magical elements. The four stories in "Her Supernatural" give us rare and otherworldly events in the lives of the female subjects. They are odd, eerie tales, curious and frightening, sad or deadly. One is even comical and sweet with whimsy.

The young girls and women are presented in a range of situations as the supernatural exerts its power, and the tales gain momentum.

WHO YOU!

ONE WAY-BACK DAY, in a reach among the hills, lay a lowland shady. And in this hollow was a cabin all by itself.

In the cabin was a whole hum and sigh of younger and elder women. Even a few her-younguns was there, too. All of them, just in there talking and tittering back and forth. It was a whole lot of shaking and laughing of her-elders and her-youngers, hair gray or light-colored, and long black dresses, all, the way they look. They made over each other, said nice things, too. They were friendly, mostly, like sisters to one another.

Suddenly, there came a knocking at the door. The elders knew the knocking had to be some poor stranger, bone hungry and tired.

"Stranger, with so little weight from not eating so much," one of the youngers whispered to an elder.

An elder whispered back, "Stranger, floating on thin air, so skinny, looking for a handout."

The her-women and girls giggled about the stranger, but they didn't let on that they had heard knocking. "Knocketoo, knocketoo," it sounded like. Almost gentle.

The women never went near the door. They wouldn't let the few young-uns near, either. They kept on, just full of themselves. And they sat there around the fire, rocking and smoking their pipes. They told *tells* on one another and on their kinfolk, don't you know. They passed gossip along about people they didn't like and about nearly everyone else. They even got to talking about each other when one of them had to leave the little sitting room for a minute or two.

"Dora been putting on weight where she can't see, but we sure can!" And they'd giggle and shake at Dora's expense.

Right then, there came a "knockata, knockata" at the door.

The women rocked, "crickety, crackety." They heaved themselves up to cook the supper. Some baked the bread. Some made the stew.

"Knockety, knock-knock," came from the door.

The women paid it no mind. They didn't pause, didn't think about who was there. They gave nary a peek at the door.

Next, the women sat down at table. They ate until they ate up every bit of food but for some dry dough on the breadboard.

"KNOCK! KNOCK!" came loud, like that.

The her-elders stuck up their noses at the noise. Some may have been part deaf. Still, the her-youngers had to hear all that knocking. "KNOCK! KNOCK!" Loud enough to wake the dead. Nobody asked, "Who's there?" Or, "Is somebody hungry?" Her-elders in their long dresses leaned back, relaxed. "Who wants to cook for you?" they asked, laughing.

Other side of the door, they hear, "Please give me a piece of bread."

The knocking been going on for some time now. Soon, the women began feeling nervous. But they were bold enough to say, "We cook for our own selves. But who is going to cook for you?"

The door came back with, "KNOCK-ETY, KNOCK-ETY." And real angry loud, too. Until all the women found they were shaking. It came so fast on them. They were scared! They heard, "Knocketu, knocketu," soft and low.

One her-younger, Benna, couldn't take much more. Her hands flew up; her arms waved. "That's just it," she said. "I've had about enough." She took up a bitty piece of dough. She patted it warm while the skillet heated. She dropped that dough in the hot skillet where it popped and sizzled.

Well, all the women looked ashamed now, since they had left the stranger only that little piece of dough. They moved around the room, throwing up their hands and waving their arms down again. They couldn't stand to look at one another, they felt so bad. And they flapped their arms, blinked their eyes, as if trying to see behind themselves.

That piece of dough swelled up so — the lid lifted right off the skillet. The dough came hard on top and smelled strong. Well, it split the skillet apart. And the dough baked into bread so fast it rolled around on the hearth, and it rose high on up the chimney. It rolled itself out on the floor, lifting up and rising higher and higher.

The women were frightened. They jumped up on the chairs. They perched up there and held their skirts up and their arms akimbo, with elbows way out and shoulders way back.

The bread climbed over the chairs. The women had to scramble up on the chair backs. Saying, "OOOh, OOOh!" They did!

All this time, the knocking is keeping on. Real low sound, "Knockatum. Knockatum."

The elder women were too afraid to look at one another. They all were so scared and ashamed of themselves for being so selfish. They hopped up and down, and hopped around, making funny clucking sounds in their throats. They blinked their eyes and kept turning their heads this way and that. All the while, the bread was swelling, rolling, and rising higher around them. Now they seemed to hear voices coming from everywhere:

> *"You do not give me, you will not lend.*
> *You abuse your neighbor, you misuse your friend.*
> *Hush up tale-telling, quit that talk.*
> *No more will you have the strength to walk!"*

At once, the women's legs became so weak they could barely step. They blinked and felt more ashamed of themselves! Couldn't look at each other; they turned their heads clear around. They quarreled deep in their throats, clucking. And from outside they heard:

> *"You wouldn't open the door*
> *To a one so hungry and poor.*
> *Fly out a window any one of you sees.*
> *Go live out your days in the hollow trees."*

Now the bread had risen so high that only chink openings were left at the tops of the windows. The women pushed each other, trying to get away. Each feared she'd be left behind.

They flew out the window chinks. As they went, each and every one of them turned into an owl. Her-elders and her-youngers and her-younguns found hollow trees to live in.

They will stay owls until they forget all the bad things they know about

folks. But till right now, they still talk about one another. Till yet, you can hear them calling from tree hole to tree hole:

"Go home, Benna! Go home, Leddie!
Oh, why don't you all go home?
You! You!"

An elder calls:

"You! Who you!
Go home! Go home yourself, Mattie Lou!"

And till tomorrow, not one of them owl women can go home.

COMMENT: This is a *pourquoi* (why) story about how owls came to be; it is a cautionary tale of the *chantefable* (cante fable) type and a transformation story. It was collected from black slaves and written down in the manner of Joel Chandler Harris's *Uncle Remus* stories, in the so-called "Negro Dialect," which was considered quaint in the storytelling period one hundred to one hundred and fifty years ago.

In the so-called "Negro Dialect," in which the tale was written, the part where the women become owls reads: "Des as dey flew out, ev'y one turnt to a owl. Ev'y one hatter go find a holler tree ter live in. Dey gotter stay owls twel day forgit all de ill dat dey know 'bout y' and o'her folks."

The "Who You!" text is here recast into ordinary colloquial speech to make reading and telling a great deal easier. The moral of this tale seems to be: Do unto others. The transformation from women to owls — or any birds — is unusual for African American supernatural tales. Most transformation stories are about men. Although women come out the worse in this one, it is still a magical story with a fairy-tale quality.

MACIE AND BOO HAG

I CAN'T GET sleep to come to bed with me no more. If and when I do drop off, it don't feel very natural.

I dream that every morning Crow comes into my pea patch and takes every single pea away in his beak. I can see my eats leaving the house with nobody's hand touching them. I see my poor mother; she, so restless in her grave. I see so many things like that. There won't be any snoring good with boo hag all the time riding me!

I was a youngun the first time boo hag rode me. I suspect some jealous girl put the hag up to it. Some young woman didn't like the young men come to court me because I was so pretty. And she wasn't nothing much, too. One boy she liked cared for me best, and so this girl put the hag on me.

One evening, boo hag come to see me. I was ready for bed early, for I was younger then. Halfway up the stairs, this green light comes, *swoosh*! And burst all in my eyes. Then it turns into a red light. I can see this awful, raggedy-looking thing coming up the stairs behind me. The she-thing has a head big as a barrel with bloody-red light shining out of her eyes. My mouth is open to scream, but I can't yell a thing. I moan some, is all I can do. And my dear mother heard me.

She came over to the landing, said to me, "Macie, what's wrong? What's the matter?"

I tried to answer, but something had locked my jaw. Couldn't even turn around to look at her. She knew there was something the matter with me.

"Must've played with bad girls again," she said.

Couldn't say nothing back to her, my mouth was just so closed. That's what boo hag did to me, made me speakless.

And the hag rode me, and I liked to died. I got real thin, she rode me so many late nights. Just like I was some broomstick she rode. Or some skinny night-mare. A whole month of nights, and I couldn't sleep a wink. That's how boo hag did me, and scared me so. And in the night-riding, I see all kinds of bad things. See the devil. See boo daddy, too. And come the dayclean, I'm so sore on my back, like somebody been beating me with a stick.

My mother said to me, "Macie, I have a mind the hag is riding you, even though you can't say. I got a way to fix the hag, break her spell so she stays fixed, too. You go to sleep now, Macie. And when you wake up, you will feel real better, for true."

Well, I did as my mother said. She gave me a potion, and I slept sound. But it seemed I could hear and see my mother beside me, where she stayed all night. And before the cock crowed, Mother saw me stir and saw me heave as the hag got ready to ride me.

My mother took up this little bottle with a cork in it, set there beside

her foot. She took the cork out of the bottle. She held the cork while she put the bottle mouth down on my stomach.

Then, Mother found her some needles. She counted thirty-three, not one more nor less. She lifted the bottle so quick, can't hardly see her hand. She threw one needle in the bottle, fast as lightning. And she corked that bottle and put thirty-two needles in the cork. This, before boo hag knew what terrible trouble she was in.

And the hag was clean gone. And stayed gone as long as I didn't give that bottle away.

And when I woke up the next dayclean? There was my nerve all back in me. The spell boo hag had over me was melted off me. Oh, did I eat some breakfast! Had me half a loaf of bread and a whole pot of gravy!

For a long time, I was careful as could be. One time, an old woman wanted to borrow some salt, but I talked through the door. Said, "No, ma'am, we all out of salt." I knew it was boo hag come after me again. Scared me to my bones. But you saw how my mother caught that hag spirit in the bottle the way she knew how. You see, she pinned it down in the bottle with that needle. And in case the hag could tear loose, she put those needles through the cork. For it's known that boo hag can't get past some sharp needles all lined up against her.

And if I should give anything to that hag voice on the other side of the door, then she might try hard to get her spirit back out the bottle, don't you know. And once she had hold of her spirit, boo hag could slip off her skin and fly all over the place, too. Ride you in just the shape of her while her skin hang there behind the door! 'Tis true!

But that's how my dear mother caught the boo hag. Yes, it was. Now, Mother is long in her grave. And now, boo hag comes back in my old age.

I don't sleep so good these days. Nowadays, this people generation don't know the tricks, and lack knowing the way my mother knew.

Well, I know how to deal with some ghost. With some ghost, you just throw a hard remark at them, and they vanish. But I tell you, you never have some rest; you always worry about getting weak after the hag has ridden you. And I am down so far these times. I am feeling fearful and tired, all of my days. I wish for my dear mother. I do.

COMMENT: This is a poignant tale out of South Carolina about a woman who fears the boo hag will bother her in her waning years. Tales about flying witches are worldwide; the modern version of the witch on a broomstick flying across the moon at Halloween is well known. Of course, the most famous flying witch was Mother Goose!

Some black tellers believe that a boo hag is the disembodied spirit of a woman who practices witchcraft. Others say a boo hag is more powerful than a common witch. They say hags are out-of-body spirits of mean, jealous living people. In the story, Macie cannot scream because boo hag has the power to swallow her voice. Boo hag will stop to count every straw in a broom, every hole in a sieve, and as many needles as can be placed in the cork of a bottle. By the time she's finished, dawn will break to stop her wickedness. For she dare not be seen by the light of day.

Chalmers S. Murray was the collector of this story for the South Carolina Writers' Project, 1935–1941. The collection was gathered by writers in the Works Progress Administration (WPA), a former federal agency (1935–1943) charged with carrying out public works to relieve national unemployment. Writers fanned out across the United States to write down the folklore of the people. "Macie and Boo Hag" was told to Mr. Murray by a black woman who said she knew a hag had ridden her. She was seventy-nine years old when she told him the story. Her name was not recorded.

LONNA AND CAT WOMAN

PRETTY POLLY was to marry young Samuel from way up the road. But there was a girl name of Lonna, said that Samuel belonged to her. She said Polly had tricked him, and she was going to get him back.

She went to the conjure woman named Cat Woman. Fear her! Woman had money to burn. She had the power. Everybody knew about her, and most stayed away from her. For her life depended on something all of us have but few of us will sell.

Lonna had got the word that Cat Woman would help her. But first, Lonna had to give Cat Woman *a suck of her blood.*

Cat Woman, she of the albino skin, was a *her-vampire.* And she fooled Lonna, said she needed her blood to make the charm against pretty Polly most powerful. "It won't be much, Lonna-girl," Cat Woman said.

She forced her sharp teeth into Lonna's neck and sucked her fill. I'm telling you true!

Afterward, Lonna went on home, dragging her legs as limp as a dishrag.

And Cat Woman hadn't even taken some money. She'd told Lonna to buy some food with it and fill her belly.

"When they lay away that Polly-girl," murmured Cat Woman (never did talk loud), "you come back for a charm. It will bring your Samuel closer to you than a sick puppy to a warm fire." Cat Woman laughed. They say the sound of her laughter came off a breath that had no life to it. Only death and darkness.

When Lonna got home, she lay down at once and could hardly lift her head from the pillow. But she was satisfied. Soon pretty Polly grew sick and tired, and took to bed. The rumor was that Polly wouldn't ever have old bones in her body.

Young Samuel was frantic over Polly. The doctor came to look at her. He said there was nothing he could see. From then on, Samuel knew the worst. He knew that Lonna had put a spell on Polly.

Samuel went to the city to find the conjure woman Lonna had gone to. He would pay for a better spell than Lonna's.

Word about the her-vampire Cat Woman was on the street. Samuel found out where she lived. She opened the door just as he was about to knock. She had on a white turban and a white gown. Her face was covered in rice powder, to hide its foul-smelling rot.

Samuel felt his flesh creep. Said the her-vampire's arms moved like bird's wings opening and shutting on a warm day. Her nails would sheathe and unsheathe like a cat's claws.

"But it was her eyes," Samuel said, later. "They bulged out at you, wet-shiny, like marble."

She told him, "I know why you come here, but I want to hear you say it."

Then Samuel told her about pretty Polly's poor state of health.

The her-vampire murmured, "My price for saving her is a suck of your young blood. Are you willing to pay the price?"

"You can get as much blood as you want from the slaughterhouse," he told her.

"I want it strong and fresh from young veins." She grinned at him. It was then Samuel saw her pointed cat's teeth.

She led him to her couch. "I was most hypnotized," he was to say. She sat down beside him, her arms around his chest. He felt her teeth break the skin on his neck, and sink in. She seemed to purr then as she sucked his blood.

After she drank her fill, she told him, "Your girl will be well by the time you get home. Just remember, I can *spell* her whenever I want. You will come back here many times to give me more blood. Don't forget."

Samuel barely made it home. But he found Polly sitting in a chair and eating everything in sight.

Meantime, Lonna was beside herself; she'd heard Polly was well. And though Lonna stuffed herself like a pig, she seemed to be drying up into an old hag. So she dragged herself to Cat Woman's door. She fussed at Cat Woman for not taking care of her. She got sassy with the her-vampire! Why'd she have to do that?

Cat Woman grabbed her and shook her like a wet rag. Lonna fainted. Cat Woman thought she'd broken her neck. She lost her head, sent for the him-vampire. Between them, they carried Lonna to the canal to dump her.

A policeman happened by, and saw them. The him-vampire took off. Other po-lice couldn't catch him. They managed to hold onto Cat Woman; she went to jail and was given no bail out. The circuit judge wasn't due for a while.

The newspapers had all the pictures of her, just awful to see. Yet the story ended just about the way you'd expect. Lonna got well, but she never tried any more nonsense over pretty Polly.

Pretty Polly went courting her Samuel, and baking cakes and pies with her mama, and roasting turkey and hog. Goodness.

And the her-vampire, Cat Woman? In the end, she stayed in jail so long she had no way to get blood. She died, of course. People said it was foolish to mess with a poison weed. Said just pull it up, and throw it in the sun, and let the roots die.

Cat Woman, the her-vampire, was sent back to the Bad she come from. And good riddance.

♀♀♀♀♀

COMMENT: This her-vampire tale may be the only one of its kind. For bloodsuckers — man, woman, or child — are rare in African American stories. But not voodoo women and conjuration.

The setting for the story is the west bank of the Mississippi River. It is the levee country forty miles south of New Orleans. The time period is not long after the Civil War but before the splitting up of the area's large sugar plantations. New Orleans was famous for its Vodu, or conjure women, such as Marie Laveau, who was the most powerful of the New Orleans voodoo queens.

Voodoo, also known as Vodun, is a religion derived from Africa and religious cult worship. The her-vampire in the above tale is described as a conjure woman, one who deals in magic spells and voodoo.

MALINDY AND LITTLE DEVIL

ONCE UPON a time, when geese were pigs, and turkeys danced the barnyard jigs, there lived a child, Malindy. She just loved to sing and dance. Everywhere she went, she sang about it — *"I'm going to get me some milk from the moo-moo-cow"* — and she would sway this way and that, to and fro.

One time, Malindy had her pail full of warm milk right from the cow, and she was going home along the fence line. *"I'm going home to supper. I've got my milk pail by my side!"* she sang. Just then, she tripped on a rough place on the path. The pail spilled milk all over the ground and all over Malindy, too.

Malindy sat there weeping, staring at that rickety-crickety fence and singing, *"Oh, boo-hoo, poor me. Now Papa will punish me. And I get no supper, too. Boo-hoo-hoo!"*

Something came along on the topmost rail of the fence. It was fuzzy-furry all over; it had a long tail.

"You, baboon," Malindy said, sniffling. "What are you doing way out here?"

Baboon didn't say anything because it wasn't any. Malindy saw then that what she thought was an animal had a pitchfork.

"I know you," she said. "You're a devil!" She started blubbering hard again, but she wasn't crying over her spilt milk, no she wasn't.

"Now, now," the devil said. "Don't take on so. I wouldn't hurt you."

At that, Malindy stopped crying. "You're a tiny fellow," she said. For the devil looked to be the size of a slender monkey.

"They call me Little Devil," he said. "But I know how to change." He grew to giant size, blotting out the trees.

"Goodness!" said Malindy. "You are truly something awful!"

"That, I am," said Little Devil. "But listen. I'm just starting out with devilment. This is my first case with a child. And I want to help you."

"I'm listening," Malindy said.

"I'll restore your milk to its pail for a price," he told her.

"Will you dry my dress off, too? My mama will spank me for getting my dress all dirty," Malindy said.

"I can do that," said Little Devil. "But first, you must promise to give me your soul when you pass beyond this earth."

"But I want to stay here a long time," said Malindy.

"How long?" asked Little Devil.

Malindy thought about it. She wanted to be as old as her mama someday. "Twenty-nine years!" she hollered, and she did a little dance.

"I can do that for you, Malindy," said Little Devil. "I'll restore your milk and fix your dress like new. I'll give you twenty-nine years, and at the end of that time, you will give me your soul."

"It's a deal!" said Malindy.

"Let's dance!" said Little Devil, and they did. They swung and swayed up and down the path.

Right then, the pail stood upright. It was full of warm milk. And *poof*! Malindy's dress was dry and looked brand-new.

"Whoo-whee!" shouted Malindy. She did a twirling dance in her sandals as Little Devil spun her just so.

Well, the time went by and went by. Soon, the twenty-nine years had gone. Malindy was grown now, with children of her own. She'd forgot all about Little Devil, such a good time she'd had. One morning, there was a commotion in the air around her. Everything turned black and red and all bright day. A loud voice hollered, "I'm going to come after you. I'm coming after you. Right now!" And lo and behold, there was Little Devil standing before her, looking just like himself.

"I remember you, no bigger than a minute," said Malindy. "How you doing?"

"Doing all right. But I come for your soul. You promised," said Little Devil.

"I remember, I did," said Malindy. "Wait a minute, I'll get it for you."

She turned her back to him. Tore off the sole of her shoe! Turned around and gave her *sole* to him.

"This it?" asked Little Devil.

"Sure is," said Malindy.

"I thought it would be bigger," he said.

"That's it," she said.

So the ugly little devil had to take her sole to his master. He didn't know any better, too.

And Malindy? Well, she went dancing along through life. So did her many children. They all lived happily ever after. See, because the devil can get your *sole* but one time. After that, he has to quit.

That's all.

COMMENT: Versions of this tale dating back to 1890 are found in Virginia, the Carolinas, and Georgia. Southern black folktellers had much to say about ghosts and devils. Having become Christians in America, they acquired the personal devil of Christianity. However, the idea of guardian spirits, and spirits in and around everything, is African in origin. The air could well be full of spirits. Notice that in the story, the air around Malindy changes colors, thus signaling an other-world presence.

In the lighthearted "Malindy and Little Devil," the heroine is a young girl. And the single-person devil, or the personal devil, comes directly from Sunday-school teachings and her family's belief in God, and in Christianity.

There is a trace of legend here, back to the Middle Ages, to the story of a Dr. Faustus, the magician said to have sold his soul to the devil in exchange for knowledge and power.

In our story, the outcome is amusing. The tale uses the play on like-sounding words (soul, sole) for comical effect.

HER FOLKWAYS
AND LEGENDS

BEYOND FAIRY TALES, animal tales, and supernatural tales, African American folklore provides a rich and varied American treasure of traditional beliefs, legends, customs, and the ways of humanity, on Earth and in the afterworld.

The tales in "Her Folkways and Legends" represent the black female's longing for an untethered position in the world. The stories reflect her high regard for freedom and equality. She wants adventure and to live as she chooses, and to have privacy and respect for her character.

WOMAN AND MAN STARTED EVEN

GOD CREATED Woman and Man. He made their house and all its doors. When Woman and Man talked together, they said the same number of words. When they fought, they also came out even. Woman was as strong as Man, don't you know. She couldn't win over him, and he couldn't beat her. That was the way it was. Just level.

"I have to see God about this," said Man. "I'm getting weary with having a woman around that I can't even whip."

So Man carried himself up to Heaven. And there, he found him, great God. "My dear God," Man said, "I come to you because you are the most, and I need help. Please, will you give me strength to win over Woman? If you make me harder and tougher, I will keep everything in place on Earth, including that woman. She thinks she's so smart and so mighty."

"Well, all right, then," says God. "I like a man knows what he wants. Now here, I give you more strength than Woman."

So Man is stronger. And he hurried home to tell Woman. "I been up in Heaven," he told her. "God given me more strength, and now I am best, and I am over you with more strength than you will ever have."

Woman was upset. "I'm going to see about this," she muttered.

She waited a whole day, getting her mind in hand. Then she went up to Heaven. "My God," she said, "I come here to get me my strength that I had one time."

"You still got the strength you had one time," says God. "It's just that Man has got some more than you."

"Well, why is that, Lord?" she asked the great God.

"Well, because he came up here and asked for some more, and I gave it to him."

"But can you give me some more, too?" asked Woman. "Or take away what you given him, so we'll be even again?"

"I can't take back what I have given," said the Lord. "You'll just have to get along with Man being the strongest."

So Woman went on her journey home. She was steaming mad at the great God. Which is the way the devil finds how to get into someone's life. And he was standing next to Woman, smiling at her. She told the devil all that happened.

He says to her, devil says, "This is how you do better than Man. You climb upstairs again. Ask God for the keys hanging by the left pearly gate. Bring them to me, and I'll let you know what comes next."

So Woman does it. She goes back up there.

"What is it you want with me this time?" God says. Getting a little tired of her busting in on him.

"Great God," Woman says. "You the big head of Heaven and Earth and all the stars."

"What is it that's on your mind, Woman?" God asks. He's getting irritated now.

"Please, give me those keys hanging by the left pearly gate."

"Well, take them," God says, "and kindly leave me alone!"

So Woman takes them and gets on down the stairs as fast as she can. There's the devil, waiting on the bottom step.

"Those are some *power* keys you got there," he tells Woman. "Take them home and lock the door to the kitchen. Lock the door to the bedroom. Lock the children's room, too."

"Why do you want me to do these things, locking up everywhere?" Woman wants to know.

"Because," says the devil, "first lockup, Man always got his stomach on his mind. Always wanting to eat up everything. Second lockup, Man has to have his sleep and gets upset when he don't have it. Third lockup, Man can't stand to be separated from his baby children. He has care about his name going on through the next generation."

So Woman hurries home. When Man comes in from his chores, she's waiting for him. Rocking on the porch and singing songs, one after the other.

Man sees that the doors are locked up tight when they are supposed to be open wide. He storms up and tries to get through. It takes all his strength, but he can't open those doors.

"Who locked up?" he yells at Woman. "Where'd you get some keys to lock up everything?"

Woman says, "God gave them over to me."

Man goes up to God, tells God what Woman said.

"Yes, well, she asked, and I gave," said God. "And that fallen angel of mine, the devil, he showed her how to use them."

"Well, give me some keys so I can get the doors open," said Man. "God, don't let her have it over me!"

"No, sorry, Man, can't do it," said the Lord. "What I give over, I don't take back, you know that. Just go ask Woman to open the doors, if you have to have them open."

Well, Man did that. But he couldn't sway Woman. Only way she would unlock the doors is when he did what she wanted.

"I got a plan," he said to Woman one day. "Let's us each take an equal part. You give me two of those keys, and I'll give you half my strength. How's that?"

"Hmmm. I have to think about it," she told him.

Woman is thinking and thinking when the devil is there rocking with her. "Woman, if I were you, I'd tell Man no," says the devil. "Let him have his strength, and you keep all the keys. And if one time you feel you might give in, remember this: When horseflies worry the horse, the horse is happy to have its hairy tail to swish them off his hide!"

Woman kept her keys. She wouldn't trade for Man's strength. So that's the way it is. Man is strong. But it's Woman who has the power.

ჶჶჶჶჶ

COMMENT: "Woman and Man Started Even" is an African American *pour-quoi* (why) tale with the rare outcome of the woman winning. It is a moral tale showing that the Almighty treats Man and Woman equally. It also reveals that the devil can enter into human concerns when people express anger toward God. Thus, the devil will upset the balance to suit himself when human beings allow him to enter their lives. The teller concedes that Woman has the power over Man. The subtle meaning is that Woman is not to be

trusted, since her power comes from the help of the fallen angel, the devil. And only with help could she ever be more powerful than Man.

This tale is widely circulated in Tennessee and is in the collection of the Tennessee Writers' Project, 1940. It was collected by James Aswell, the collection's editor.

The test of any good folktale is how long it stays in the minds of listeners and in circulation with tellers. It is meant to be humorous, of course. This tale begs to be told and retold.

LUELLA AND THE TAME PARROT

ONE TIME, not yours or my time, but it was a bygone time, some people was owned. And the owners were called Mistress and Master by the people was owned. And no matter what, even when they had gone to meeting, the owners always knew what the owned, the slaves, were doing. The slaves might stop for an hour in the fields to pray, and they weren't allowed to pray. But they did because the Master and Mistress were away, couldn't see them.

But the owners did too see them praying there down on their bendings. But we didn't know how they saw us, because they weren't nowhere to be seen. But they saw us anyhow. Maybe we'd taken an extra chicken in the winter when we 'most starved to death. And they would know we had it hidden under the bed. We children played with Mistress's daughters. And we'd sneak away from them sometimes in the day. We'd sneak back into our cabin and crawl under the bed and get some secret chicken to eat from the pan there. That was the only good food we could have to eat. The rest all the time was neck bones, if we were lucky. Just greens most times, if we were not.

But one day, Luella was working in the house upstairs, and she hears the Mistress's bird, that green parrot, a-talking away. She thought it was some woman with a croaking voice up there.

She goes in, and there is the parrot in a cage just talking to itself. Just under some spell. Saying things, just going on about what they'd been doing. "Let us pray," it said. "I want some more chicken." "Chicken's under Sadie's bed." "Don't let Master know we are here resting."

Well, Luella went and told all them who were owned about the tame parrot that could talk. Everybody wanted to hear, didn't believe her, at first. But when they heard that bird squawking, "Can I have some hoppin' John, please?" they knew it was the truth. They all had to toe the line then. Couldn't mess around, less they did it in silence, and that was hard to do. They cut down on their playtime, then.

One time the owner went to a neighbor's in his buggy with Mistress and come on back and asked the tame parrot what he'd heard and seen. Parrot say, "Don't know. I went blind and deaf the whole day."

Luella had put a black hood over its head!

COMMENT: The tale of the parrot telling on the slaves has many versions and is widespread. The secret to the owner knowing all is, of course, that the parrot repeats what it hears. The last part, when the parrot is asked what it's heard and seen, is a tall tale. A parrot cannot make up its own answer to a question. But here its answer is humorous and makes a good story. All the variants to the tale end in similar fashion, with the parrot saying it was deaf, or in a closet, or in Hell, or blind.

Such stories as this that slaves told on themselves, which were usually told by a female teller, lightened the heavy burden of their lives in bondage.

THE MER-WOMAN OUT OF THE SEA

OUR COUNTRYSIDE stretches along the ocean. Our city is full of life. We have the best of field crops and of food from the sea. Our younguns can read and write, laugh and sing. We have the best of good, and even better. We sleep deep and long in the nighttimes, as calm as babies.

But one day, something let loose at us out of the blue. A black cloud the size of a man's hat started way up high. We all saw it swell until it filled up the whole sky. Then, it came swirling straight down on our shoulders like some giant, scaresome boil, ready to burst.

Rain upon rain fell from the rolling black cloud. Its darkness bullied down our streets. Lightning streaked past our windows; thunder cracked. We cringed, covered our heads for dear life. It rained rivers over our roofs and down our chimneys.

All at once, the wind of it died down. The lightning of it emptied out of the air. No thunder sounded. Rain fell as steady as every day and every night. We felt the rain would never stop.

Days passed, and the whole of our city became a flood, far and wide.

Every road was a marshland. Every reach of land was a lakeland. In the woods, the trees gave off an odor of rot. All kinds of garbage and muck floated in the streets, clear to our knees. Cockroaches emptied out of our kitchen walls by the thousands — into the flood, and up our backs! What had been hard ground under us became soft and squishy, like flesh wet and fallen off the bone. Some of us folks went crazy.

Rain came down for four, five weeks. All of us became jittery with nerves. We felt there was something new and never seen among us. We'd all heard this tale, that something drenched and cold had crawled out of the sea. It made its way overland, through the rot and stench of wet.

The dark rumor spread among our houses. A woman screamed it, clawing at the lampposts: "There's a mer-woman among us! Yes, A *mermaid*! Our city is drowned. The water will claim us all unless *She* is put back to sea."

That was the story we all believed. We were hysterical. Damp all the time, the sky ghostly dark every day, we'd believe anything. It was the mermaid that caused our misfortune.

We all knew who had captured the mermaid. It was the doctor, with his roots and potions. He was our druggist, our apothecary, as he was known in past times. We all knew him, but we stayed away from him. Because he was the doctor to the dead things; for years, that was the whispered report. He had a hidden room of otherworldly creatures, so the story went. Terrible, half-alive things that ought not to have seen the light of day, ever, some said.

This doctor of darkness had a helper — Asa was his name. He told us, whispering, "He keeps *Her* with his ungodly things. On the topmost shelf, there is a bell jar. And in the bell jar is a mer-woman being. The mermaid."

"No!" we said, but we believed. "Say it isn't true!"

"Oh, yes," Asa told. "She's a beauty. But she's shrunken down, and she's been out of her ocean too long. She's awful tiny in the tall bell jar, but she's just so lovely to see!"

"How does she seem?" we asked. "Is she all right?" We did not want her to suffer and die.

"She's covered in green water," Asa told. "She has long hair that floats and waves around her. Hair looks just like stringy vines in a breeze. Her mouth is open. Fists, banging on the bell-jar sides. She wants out!"

"No! Oh, no!" we said.

"And there are goldfish swimming in there, round and round her, too," Asa told.

Oh, we believed, all right. That this doctor to deadly things of life held a mermaid captive in a tall bell jar.

The rain kept on. It beat down on our porches and into our windows. It emptied into our rooms and fireplaces. It seemed that all at once we got angry. We were tired of it all! Of sitting in our chairs, with water up to our knees. We stormed; we raged. And finally, we gathered and became a great mob, wading out toward our doctor's shop. We were sodden and wild with fear.

We picked up the muck in our hands, throwing it at our doctor's window.

"Bring us the mermaid!" we shouted. Yes! The thought of her there made us sad enough to cry. "We say let her out, let her go back to where she belongs!"

"But there's no such thing!" called the doctor. "There is no mermaid here or anywhere."

"You lie!" one tall black man shouted.

A very small man bravely swam down to a basement window. He was gone a long time. Then, we heard things breaking. Next came putrid, slithering, crawling things out of the house. Their slime coated the waters where we stood cringing.

The small dark man floated up, breathless. "I've seen her!" he gasped. "She's got her little hands on the rim of her jar. She's crying. I tell you, she is beyond beautiful, the tiny, pitiful thing."

Some men of our town got together. They broke down the door and searched the shop — upstairs, downstairs, and in secret places. The rest of the horrible, half-living things must have hidden in deep, dank corners. For our men found nothing unusual. No mermaid at all.

"We give you our word. There is no such thing here," they told us. "Go on home."

A tall white man said to us, "If you don't leave at once, we'll call out the army to make you leave." Speaking that way to us, who've lived in this city all our lives!

The mer-woman was never found. Some of us had hoped to hold her on our palms and talk to her, too. Maybe if those men had just reached up to the top shelf over there, or in the shadows behind things in the doctor's back room, they'd've seen the mermaid swimming, swimming in her jar. Likely she'd shrunk to the size of a baby frog, and a hungry one, too. She'd been there all along, but so shriveled they couldn't recognize her.

The rains did stop, perhaps because the bell jar was now big enough to suit the mermaid. Or else the doctor to the dead things was so frightened by what he'd done, he'd sent her out the back way. Down the flooded streets and woods and on to her home at the bottom of the ocean. We knew she'd caused the rains; we didn't blame her. We blamed the doctor!

Well, what had been was gone, once the rain ended. All that was left when the waters went away to where they belonged was a stinking, rotten fish smell. And lots of muck for us in the city to clean up. Our streets smelled as if tons of fish had been cleaned on our stoops and in our houses.

For weeks, we washed down our walls, and scrubbed and swept our streets. We tried hard to rid ourselves of souring fish odors. On hot days, you can still smell them.

Our doctor soon closed his shop and moved away, some say to the north. We've not heard from him. Maybe he is dead, but no one here can say. Still, we all know that men live, and then they die. All the time. And maybe mer-women, mermaids, do as well.

COMMENT: This is a tale of such amazing detail that it takes on legendary proportions. The original story gives the exact date of the event: July 3, 1867. The description is vivid enough for the storm to have happened.

Indeed, John Bennett, who collected this tale around the turn of the century, had details of the story corroborated by a local black woman. Her name was Araminta Tucker, who told him, "It rained for thirty days, then the town rose. Oh, my God, how it rained!"

Black seagoing families lived along the South Carolina coastal area around Charleston where the tale takes place. There, the weather often was wild and frightening. After a storm, all manner of debris washed up onshore. This type of story about mermaids, while rare, comes from sea experience and the free imaginations of African American tellers.

Martha Bennett Stiles, the granddaughter of Mr. Bennett, has written to say that this retelling of her grandfather's tale, and others from his collection, "would have been of great satisfaction to him, as it was just what he collected the stories for."

ANNIE CHRISTMAS

BLACK FOLKS tell about Annie Christmas, and so do white folks. Every kind of folk claim her as their own, and there are good reasons why. But let *me* tell you. Who am I? I am the kind of grandmaw that lives to spin a good yarn.

Annie Christmas was coal black and tree tall. She stood seven feet barefoot, and she weighed two-ninety-nine pound. She would tell you she was the biggest woman in the state of Loo'siana, the strongest that ever lived in New Orleans-town. She was a keelboat operator up and down the Mississippi, and she knew New Orleans-town like the back of her hand. She dressed like a man, in harsh men's clothes. She had a mustache, too. She could make fists hard, and she would fight boatmen by the dozen and beat them down every time.

Oh, men were stone scared of Annie 'cause she was tough. They say her baby sons were born one after the other for twelve days, but I don't know about that. Yes, twelve sons she had, and they were just as night-black as she was.

I'll tell you about the time Annie decided to dress up like a fine lady. She shaved that mustache real close so it wasn't there. She piled her raven hair up and stuck peacock feathers in it. She sashayed around in this shiny, purple outfit. Then she and a bunch of her dressed-up girlfriends took a day trip on her keelboat on that 'ole, evil Mississippi River. Well, they say that big, flowing fury and the devil is step-brothers, can't stop warring each other, but I don't know.

Every time Annie's boat moored at a landing, one of her girlfriends had a gentleman waiting. A date, they call 'em now. In my day, we called them boys dandies, all fussy and overstuffed in their shirts and scarlet bow ties. "So long, Annie," a girlfriend would call back and wave. "Have a swell time!" Annie would be left with one less guest on her keelboat outing.

By the time they reached a landing downriver, Annie was completely alone. All the girls had gone with their dates. So Annie hitched her keelboat to a side-paddle-wheel boat heading for New Orleans-town. She got on the paddleboat just like any lady, and she had a good old time all by herself. Just being on a fine old boat, a-chugging along. Just feeling the breeze in her face and cooling her down. That was Annie, too, able to enjoy the simple things.

Well now, the captain of the paddleboat happened to be about as mean as they come. So was the weather that day. And as the day wore on, Annie got sassy.

"Both you better keep out my way," muttered Annie. She frowned at the darkening sky and glared at the captain. He kept away from her. That man knew who she was. Everybody up and down the devil river knew Annie.

Evening came, night came. The river was boiling and raging with the sky blooming with clouds growing high and wide, moving fast.

The Mississippi rolled over on its back and kicked and punched the devil. Next thing, the boat hit a sandbar. Annie was right there, standing behind the captain, ready to take over, but keeping quiet.

The captain shouted, raged at his crew. He swung the boat back hard — and hit another sandbar, too. This time he hollered real bad words at his crew. His clothes and face were drenched in sweat. He bellowed curses at God, and that made Annie Christmas hot and mad as a tiger.

Still, Annie did admire a strong, bad man. Something real soft came over her. Annie Christmas gave the captain her sweetest smile and said, "Give me a hug!" Couldn't help herself, poor thing. She knew a paddleboat captain was a special kind, couldn't get over one that was big and mean and strong, too.

"Oh, get outta here, you crazy woman! I'm sick of you. You are some giant bad luck, too. Get off my boat — now!" said the captain.

Well, that hurt Annie, to be put off like that. She was in love and then out of love in about a minute flat.

"I hope some big trouble gets you," she told the captain. "You'd better watch out this night. Your crew, too. For all that's bad is right with you!"

With that, Annie Christmas got on her own boat and tore out of there. But she was real saddened, some say. They say Annie couldn't get over the captain whom she'd cared about for a minute. She got dressed up in her prettiest satin dress one fine night, went out on the river, and jumped overboard. She was never seen again. Poor thing drowned like a rat.

That captain with the side-wheeler, well, he was never seen again, either, nor any of his crew. But he haunts the big devil river. You can hear him cursing the weather, the sky, and the river on nights full of rain and darkness, so folks tell.

As for poor Annie, some say her sons found her washed ashore. They wrapped her in an ebony shroud and put her in a coal-black coffin. A hearse drawn by black horses carried her to the wharf. All of New Orleans-town was there to see that hearse with six of her sons on each side. They were splendid in black — black spats and black top-hats, too; and each of them seven feet tall. Every keelboat man that ever rode the river was there to witness the somber parade. And all Annie's girlfriends. And all the men she'd beaten at hand-wrestling and fistfighting.

Darkness fell, with no moon shining. The coffin was placed on a black barge. Then her tall sons climbed aboard and floated out with the coffin clear to the sea. All of it, Annie in her coffin, the sons in their black splendor, and the barge, too, vanished from sight and were forever gone.

Now you can believe this last, or not. But this is what the black folks say. Annie Christmas is still on the big river around New Orleans-town. The black barge comes out of the mist. Her twelve sons stand straight and still, six on each side of the coffin. And there's Annie, sitting on her own wood grave, singing a river tune to the thundering sky.

COMMENT: "Annie Christmas" is one of the hometown stories of New Orleans. She is as common to southern Louisiana as is the Gumbo, the French *patois* spoken by some American blacks and Creoles — persons of mixed Spanish, French, and African ancestry who are descendants of the region's early settlers.

Many tales are told about Annie, that she was Irish or African. In the above tale, she is African American. Annie is one of the very few original model heroines, or *prototypes,* in African American folklore who is black *and* female.

Similar to John Henry, for example, she is larger than life, and legendary in that she may have been fashioned after someone who actually lived. Detailed accounts of her life make her seem quite real. Yet the drama in the vision of her twelve tall sons dressed in black, the hearse, the black coffin and black Annie in it, the black barge, all vanishing in the blackest night, is an elaborate fiction, drawn with loving, fearsome care.

There is even a questionable tale about Annie that claims there were two white writers on a New Orleans newspaper who "created" her. It's possible that they did make up a story about a white Annie Christmas. But tales about black Annie have been around for longer than anyone can remember. It's more than likely that they will continue to be told and added to.

HER TRUE TALES

NO COLLECTION of *Her Stories* would be complete without "Her True Tales." These are accounts of black women's lives told in their own voices and, as much as possible, in their own words. The accounts have been edited. I have from time to time modernized the language from the fractured, so-called black English in which collectors were fond of recording some of the stories. I have rendered this stereotyped English into an accessible, colloquial speech that changes to fit each woman's word patterns and tone more precisely. Generally, the women's words are their own and alive with their own way of telling.

Millie Evans and Lettice Boyer have passed on; unfortunately, photographs of them are not available. Mary Lou Thornton, however, is much alive, living in Ohio, and still doing good works. The true stories of these women are representative of hundreds that were collected. Beginning in the 1920s and 1930s, biographical sketches of black women were carefully recorded under various state and federal government programs established to preserve the documentary history and lore of Americans.

They are still being collected today.

MILLIE EVANS: PLANTATION TIMES

NORTH CAROLINA

MY BIRTHDAY always comes in the fodder-pulling[1] time. My mama told me she was pulling fodder until the hour before I was born. Me, born in 1849. At the time of Surrender, I was a young lady.

Don't remember the owners' names. But I remember there was about a hundred of us kind. The owners were rich. Mistress tended to us, the women. The Master took over the men.

At four o'clock each morning, he would ring the bell for us to get up. Oh, you could hear that bell all over the plantation. I can hear it now — *ting, ting-aling-aling.* I can see all us stirring, getting up in Carolina.

Mistress raised me. But I stayed with my mama every night. My mama had to work very hard. And if Mistress thought the little black children like me were hungry between the meals, she would call us up to the house to eat. We had johnnycake sometimes and plenty of buttermilk to go with it.

See, they put the buttermilk in a long trough they kept very clean. They filled the trough with buttermilk. And we little black children would get around the trough and drink into our mouths. We'd hold our johnnycake in our hands.

The cooking was always done outdoors for the black folks because there were so many of us. Greens were cooked in a black pot, the kind you wash clothes in. They'd crumble bread in the pot likker and give us spoons, and we would stand round the pot and eat.

We usually ate out of gourds and had homemade wood spoons.

Dinnertime was regular sit-down, and the table, with an oilcloth over it, was set under a chinaberry tree. Oh, and we had plenty to eat. We grew all the food, raised plenty of meat, raised sugar, rice, peas, chickens, eggs, cows.

I remember when freedom come. The Yankees said, "Free!" like that. Master didn't want to part with us, and he thought if we all went to Arkansas, he shouldn't have to send us off into what we didn't know about. We were all afraid to be free, afraid one would get gone from the other. So we loaded up all the wagons. And off we all went, all hundred of us and Mistress and Master and their children, and horses, cows, everything. We had plenty to eat and plenty of horsefeed. We traveled hard, fifteen, twenty miles a day. Camped at night and cooked enough in the morning to last us all day. We drove the cows with us.

But on the way the owner, him, died. We camped while they carried him back to North Carolina. Mistress went with him. She came on back, and we went on to Arkansas. We reached it safely, although three of the slaves died. We buried them along the way.

When we got there, we found out that freedom was already there ahead of us. It was right there, too. That was something. Mistress begged us to stay with her. She was old by then, and she soon died. We stayed until they took her back to Carolina. There wasn't none of them left but her daughter. She soon married and was gone. We lost track of the son.

Don't remember all of it from them days. But I do remember some such.

COMMENT: Miss Millie Evans would have been sixteen at the end of the Civil War in 1865. The end of the war was generally known by former slaves as the Surrender. By her own account, Miss Evans was treated fairly well and fed well as a slave. Later, she became a cook on the plantation. She was in her elder years at the time she is speaking in the 1930s. Her narrative reveals that her life of slavery was harsh. The picture of slave children eating at a trough like so many animals is shocking, and revealing. It clearly shows that the slave owners thought of the slaves as less than human. They valued slaves, of course, but only as property, animals to be worked, fed, and driven, the same as horses and cows. Obviously, the owners' knowledge of the war and Surrender was limited, since they believed they could move to Arkansas and avoid giving their slaves freedom.

This story was abridged and adapted from "Millie Evans: North Carolina" from the *Journal of American Folk-Lore*, Volume II, January–March 1889. Copyright © 1889 by the American Folk-Lore Society.

1. Fodder is coarse food for livestock, composed of entire plants.

LETTICE BOYER: FROM WAY BACK

NORTH CAROLINA

L ETTICE BOYER is my name. I'm a hundred and ten years old. My mind's clear, but my memory has come short these last ten years. Oh, I've been here from way back! I was here when Nat rose up, when the stars fell down, when the war come in, when the Surrender was, when it was the earthquake, and I'm still here.[1]

Nowadays, I can't get around nowhere without my stick. All I can do is look at folks working in the field. I'm past working. Last week my bedclothes and my apron and dress were so dirty, I had to wash them. So I filled up a tub of water; I found some more dirty clothes to put with mine. And I got out a tubful of washing on the line before my granddaughter, Hallie, come in from the field. It about did me in, too. My back hasn't been right since. All I'm fit for these days is some sweeping of the yard and patching clothes.

Witches is what ails my back. They ain't so bad nowadays, but they still rides a body at night. Once when I was down-a-bed with fever, my care-fors put ointment all over me. And this witch come in and looked hard at me. Says, "Humph! Too greasy!"

"For what?" I says. "For witches to ride me on the night?"

But to stop witches, you put a broom under the bed. Witches can't bother you before they count every straw in the broom.

Haunts? Of course there are. I've seen them, but they don't scare me. They are just dead people come back to their old range. Once a woman walked in front of me for a long time, and I could never catch up with her. She just kept the same distance, no nearer, no farther. Another time I seen a woman sitting on a stump at the side of the road. She was there as plain as my hand. Until I took my eyes off her a second when I looked again, she was gone. A haunt won't ever vanish as long as you keep your eyes on it.

The only thing I've been afraid of is the living, not the dead, and not the haunts.

Sometimes when I think about those days before the war, we was all slaves . . . I wonder if we wouldn't've been better off without freedom. Maybe not; some wanted their freedom so bad. A heap of slaves had a hard time back then.

I was born at Brandon's plantation down on the Neck.[2] My mama had twenty children. My father was made ferryman across the Roanoke River. That was his job until the Surrender.

I was raised in the great plantation house to help nurse the children and wait on the table. Every winter we got two pair of yarn stockings and two pair of winter shoes. We had summer shoes, too, and dresses, and a shaker. A shaker is a bonnet made out of wheat straw that kept our heads cool in the hot sun.

All of it changed after Miss Louise, the Mistress, died. Then the over-seers took control. When they sent me to the field, my hard times began. They whipped us there. The men were billbo'd (billboarded). Slave men had to stick their heads through a hole cut in a board. They would lie there through the beatings. Their ears were marked just like hogs.

My mama read the Bible and knew the war was coming. Bible said:

"The sun shall be darkened and the moon give no light

   and the stars from Heaven shall fall,

   and brother shall fight against brother,

   and every nation shall go to its own home

   and worship God under their own fig tree."

So when the stars begun to fall, everybody knew the war was at hand. We never found a one of them stars on the ground. But long as the war came to stay, the stars fell from the sky at night.

Well, now, all my children are dead. Nobody left but me, one grand-daughter, several great-grandchil'ren, four great-great-grandchil'ren. Hal-lie, my granddaughter, is my closest kin. Two months ago she sent her Will over to bring me to her to stay, 'cause she says I mustn't no longer be by myself.

It bothers me having to come here and put up on Hallie and Will. I've got nothing to pay them for taking me in. I have never done anything for Will. There's two children here, too, to eat off the one bale of cotton he made last year, without me causing a crowd. Sometimes when I get to table, I sit there and cry, because I'm so hungry, and I hate so bad to eat up Will's food.

"Go on and eat," Will says, "for as long as I've got bread, you have, too."

One day, I was sitting in the yard by myself. Will came out, says, "What are you doing, Granny?"

"I'm studying."

"About what?"

"Trouble."

"Don't set out there in the cold," he says. "Come to the fire."

I didn't tell him how it hurt me to sit at his fire and not even able to tote a stick of wood in. I don't know how long I'm going to live. My mama was a hundred and five when she died. I wish I could stay here until I'm a hundred and twenty. I know I will go good and see all of my folks when I die, but I'd like to live to be a hundred and twenty-five maybe, first. Do you reckon I can? I'm a hundred and ten now.

I wouldn't mind some cheese and light bread. If you bring me some, I'd sure be proud of it.

COMMENT: The beauty in the words of the storyteller is a revelation. A portion of her narrative is recast here in a mild colloquial speech (from the collector's so-called black plantation English, with de's and dats for the's and thats). The narrative outlines her life and also documents her folk beliefs and superstitions. At one point, she suggests she and other slaves would have been better off without freedom. But her view is from the depression of the 1930s when she and her relatives lived in extreme poverty. Likely she is reminded of the terrible times of hunger and disorder after Surrender. Slaves had always been commanded to do the owner's bidding and allowed no will of their own. They who formerly couldn't make a move without being told, after the war, suddenly found themselves homeless and starving, without direction, work, or money.

It is clear that the storyteller did become strong, and proud to be free and independent. Old age brought her some amount of physical pain. Her daily sorrow was that she had to depend on her kinfolk. They were good to her, but they barely had enough for themselves. It touches us that she must ask the WPA worker who is recording her story for a bit of bread and cheese.

Lettice Boyer is probably not the storyteller's real name, for names were often changed when these authentic accounts were published for the public to read. This one was collected in 1939. How many years the story-teller lived was not recorded. Yet we are fortunate to have this nearly mythic account of some of her significant time on Earth.

This story was abridged and adapted from "No Stick-Leg," as collected by Bernice Kelly Harris, in *Such As Us: Southern Voices of the Thirties*, edited by Tom E. Terrill and Jerrold Hirsch. Copyright © 1978 by University of North Carolina Press. Used by permission of the publisher.

1. Nat rose up — the Nat Turner Slave Rebellion of 1831.

The stars fell down — possibly Belias Comet, appeared in 1846.

The war come in — 1861, the Civil War.

The Surrender was — 1865 and the end of the Civil War.

It was the earthquake — Charleston, South Carolina, earthquake of 1886.

2. Far eastern North Carolina. It is a peninsula bounded by Albemarle and Pamlico Sounds.

MARY LOU THORNTON: MY FAMILY

OHIO

I WAS BORN the first of September, nineteen and fifteen. Born in Valley View, Kentucky. My family were Mundays. . . . They lived in the country. Valley View, Kentucky, was a very small place right on the Kentucky River between Richmond and Lexington. . . . And about the only important thing you could look forward to was the train going past the house every day. The most important thing to my mother was to bring us to Ohio so we could get an education.

I was nine years old when we came to Ohio. I am next to the oldest girl. The boys Chester and Earl are older, and they're still living. Willard, my brother who was also older, died here in Yellow Springs at the age of eighteen.

By the time we came to Ohio, there were six living out of thirteen of us born. And my brother died in Ohio, made seven dead. Most of them died when they were babies. I had a sister who choked to death on a marble. We lived in the country, and the doctor had to come on horseback.

By the time he got there the baby was too far gone. He didn't even tie up his horse. Ran in the house and got the marble out. Too late. She died. She was about three years old.

My mother would wake up and there'd be a baby dead in the crib. Living in the country, many things happened. You see it . . . but being young, you don't dwell on those things very much. I know I miss my brother.

I had no school hardly until we came to Ohio. I tried to go to school, but we had to ride between five and seven miles in an open wagon. The horses were malnourished horses. And the school board gave a father a certain amount of money to have his two boys transport the children to school up at Grapevine, Kentucky. We would go up to Tates Creek Pike and go across the creek to get to the Grapevine School. If we were at school and there came a big rain, then the creek was *up*. We'd still have to cross the creek to come back home. It was *very* dangerous. But we never thought about it. The horse keepers, Walker and Albert, those boys would beat those horses to get them across the creek. We'd all be in the wagon. I was eight or nine. I have a picture of that school. A country school, way off the road, a one-room school. Mrs. Twine was my teacher and was black. The principal was white.

One of the nicest things we'd have, we'd go for walks, and we had hickory nuts and berries, and nobody ever thought of snakes. Evidently I learned to read there. Because when I came to school here, the Elm Street School, I could read. Mrs. Emma Carnes was my teacher then. I was so good in the first grade that she asked me would I like to go into the second grade. Well, most teachers would have just automatically promoted you. I didn't know what it was all about. So when she asked me that, I told her, "No, I'll stay in the first grade, it was nice!"

I sat there in first grade and did second-grade work. I could write well and everything. I enjoyed everyone.

As a family, we'd entertain ourselves at home. We sang. We would all dress up and entertain our parents in the evening by having plays. I'd read to my parents and tell them about whatever books I had read. They would just *enjoy* listening to it. My mother had about a fourth-grade education, and my father had about a fifth-grade. But he was a whiz when it came to math. But they taught themselves to read the paper, to read the Bible, and they did it quite well.

When I got my first job, I was making about fifteen dollars a week. And I knew I was rich! So I bought my father a blue serge suit. He was *so* happy with it that he seldom wore it. He said he liked it so much he wanted to save it and be buried in it. So my brothers and all of us got together and bought him another suit to wear. But he kept that blue serge suit, and he *was* buried in it.

COMMENT: I have known Mrs. Thornton all of my life but never knew any of her story until she was interviewed for an oral history project conducted in 1979–1980 in Yellow Springs, Ohio.

The Munday family, now spelled Mundy, is well known in the village of Yellow Springs. Mrs. Thornton, Mary Lou Mundy, taught Sunday school when I was a child. She made sure that her charges had memorized and could recite their "pieces" at Easter and Christmas.

Mrs. Thornton is eighty years old. She is a stalwart supporter of the African Methodist Episcopal Church, the Senior Citizens Center, and the Yellow Springs village community. She remains a kind and gentle friend.

MORE ABOUT *HER STORIES*

THIS BOOK has to do with my early beginning. For it starts way back when, with my being the kind of child I was. I was the child who listened closely to grown-up women talking. To this day, I remember how my grandmother, my aunts and great-aunts and elder cousins looked when they talked. I've never forgotten how they moved their hands and gestured with their arms. The sounds of their voices and much of what they said stays with me.

When I was a child, I heard stories told by women. My mother told me the first tale I remember hearing. I didn't know it was a whimsy, a playful fancy, made up on the spot to comfort me.

A moment before my mother made up the story, our house felt as if it had gathered itself in. It braced itself; it shook and trembled, and so did I.

I was quite a little child at the time, and it seemed to me Mother and I lived in a great house all by ourselves. We were home alone all day. I had brothers and sisters, but they were off to school before I woke up in the morning. I forgot all about them until I saw them in the daylean, around four o'clock when the sun began to slant across the living room.

My father had to work until late at night. He was gone before I awoke and didn't come home until I was asleep. So I saw him mostly on weekends. But he was there in the feel of absence in the house, of silence in hallways. Yet, something of him remained with me all day, in the lumpy shape of him left in the big easy chair where he would read the paper. Sometimes, pouting, I would climb up and fit myself into the shape and try to be commanding, the way he was. I always missed my dad.

Meantime, during the day hours, my mother and I did things together. Sometimes, we climbed the stairs and went into all the rooms. I remember the sound of my mother's voice, as she busied herself with the household chores. I would be as close to her as I could get without bumping into her. Sometimes, I held onto a belt loop or her hem. She didn't mind. I paid particular attention to her face. Her eyes were so shining and dark; her lips kept their smile for me through the day.

Mother had much the same voice in her nineties as she had when I was a child. It had a lightness to it, especially when she told stories. It trembled at its edge, full of fresh tones. Even in her old age, Mother's voice never changed its crystal-clear quality, of being happy who she was and where she was. She was so gentle with me.

One day, we were upstairs, making my brothers' beds. Ours was a traditional home, where women did the household chores, and men went out into the world. But that truth only went so far. Farm women like my mother could do about anything they set their minds to. Besides taking care of her five children, Mother also raised six hundred leghorn chickens and sold eggs by the dozens to the local grocery. She grew cucumbers and tomatoes and sold them by the bushel. The money she made she called Extra. And Extra money meant new Easter coats or new school clothes for us children.

Mother killed a chicken for our supper by taking hold of its neck and twirling it around and around, until the body of the chicken broke from the neck, whirled away, and plopped to the ground. The headless chicken would hop about, until all its blood drained into the soil.

I watched my mother kill chickens that way a hundred times. It sounds cruel, I know. But chickens were the food we ate, like vegetables. What we didn't grow or raise, we didn't eat.

My brothers and sisters couldn't stand to watch Mother "ring a chicken," as we called it. Neither could my father. He would disappear somewhere until Mother took the bird into the kitchen to prepare it for supper.

This one day, Mother and I were upstairs, making the beds. "Take hold of the sheet end down there," Mother told me.

I grabbed at the sheet.

"Now you must tuck it in." But before I could, the house suddenly went still. The outdoors grew dark, like heavy shade.

"Outside took the sun away from us," Mother murmured. All at once, she stopped fluffing pillows. The house seemed to brace itself. It began to shudder and tremble. In one motion, Mother dropped pillows on the bed and reached for me.

A great howl and moan came from the dark day. Mother took me in her arms as something huge hit the house and shook it hard. And made me afraid.

"Let's look and see what's what," Mother told me. She knelt with me at the front window, back a ways, but we could still see outside.

"Oh, it's a wind all right," she said. "Look at the lilac bush." Carefully, she leaned me around and to the right, so I could look down on our lilac by the porch.

I sucked in my breath. For our great lilac was bent over nearly to the ground.

"You see that?" she asked me. "Why, Lilac's the grandmother, see? She's the oldest of all. And she says, 'Bow down!' And look at the trees — whee! See how they bow down with her? They know who she is. She's showing them. Here comes the wind!"

"Whee!" I said. Mother bowed me over. I laughed for joy. The wind howled, and all the trees I could see were bent over nearly to the ground.

The clothesline with clothes on it came flying across the yard. "Ginny, you see that?" Mother said. "Grandmother Lilac has called our shirts and petticoats to come tangle with the wind!"

I grinned and flapped my arms. I was murmuring, too, trying to say words Mother said, as she said them. The sounds we made there at the window! They were enough to take the wind out of my head. The two of us so close and warm together. And making sound, making story.

"Now the trees, they'd like to get up. But Grandmother says, 'No, not now, you just wait.' See? See? Ginny, can you see the wind?"

I looked up at her face. "No, you can't, baby!" Mother said. "But you can see what wind can do. Watch it bend those trees. And even Grandmother Lilac must bend, or she will break."

Mother smiled at me. "We don't have to bend this time. We'll be ever careful, though. Looks like we're safe inside!" She straightened, lifting me up.

We went back to the chores. Finally, the wind went away. Later, outside, Mother and I picked up clothes strewn all over.

That's all I remember of that day, when there was a cyclone, I learned later, the only one I've ever seen or heard. I remember the trees bowing down and the huge sound of wind. And the way Mother's talking, telling, made me forget my fear.

All of Mother's stories taught things, little things about life and nature. I heard the Bruh Rabbit, Tar Baby story from her. She told me the true story of my Grandfather Levi's escape from slavery in Virginia. And she said that it was the first story that she'd ever heard. Mother's were family stories — how her brother, my uncle, had been swinging with me on the porch swing moments before he got in his car and was killed on the highway.

She told about the day I was born; how she lived in Canada and had met my father there. My sister, Nina, was born in Calgary, Alberta, Canada. My mother and father together told about their lives.

But it is the women of my family I was most attuned to. All those female relatives Mother visited and who visited her. The women whose parlors and kitchens were places of safety and rest on a hot summer's day. My cousins and I knew we could escape a thunderstorm on an aunt's front porch. In winter, covered with snow, we'd bang on back doors and soon have the warmth of kitchen stoves and hot chocolate.

These women of my family were usually home and always able and willing to offer us children comfort.

We'd sip hot cider, sassafras tea, and listen in wonder to the household tales. Of course, they were gentle reminders about nature's power, about ourselves in the world, where we came from, and who we were. I knew that one day I would make a book all about women like my mother, talkers, those tale tellers, and about whom tales were also told.

There, you have it.

USEFUL SOURCES

Abrahams, Roger. *Deep Down in the Jungle . . . : Negro Narrative Folklore from the Streets of Philadelphia.* Hatboro, Pa.: Folklore Associates, 1964.

Aswell, James R., et al. *God Bless the Devil: Liars' Bench Tales. Tennessee Writers' Project.* Chapel Hill, N.C.: University of North Carolina Press, 1940.

———. *Tennessee Writers' Project.* Chapel Hill, N.C.: University of North Carolina Press, 1960.

Ballowe, Hewitt L. *The Lawd Sayin' the Same: Negro Folk Tales of the Creole Country.* Baton Rouge, La.: Louisiana State University Press, 1947.

Beckwith, Martha Warren. *Black Roadways.* Chapel Hill, N.C.: University of North Carolina Press, 1929.

Bennett, John. *The Doctor to the Dead: Grotesque Legends and Folk Tales of Old Charleston.* New York: Rinehart & Company, Inc., 1943 and 1946.

Boas, Franz, et al. *Journal of American Folk-Lore,* Volume II, January–March 1889. Published for the American Folk-Lore Society. London: Houghton, Mifflin & Co., 1889.

Brewer, J. Mason. *American Negro Folklore.* Chicago: Quadrangle Books, 1968.

Christensen, A. M. H. *Afro-American Folk Lore.* Boston: J. G. Cupples Co., 1892. Reprint, New York: Greenwood Publishing Corp., Negro Universities Press Division, 1969.

Culbertson, Anne V. *At the Big House.* Indianapolis: The Bobbs-Merrill Co., Publishers, 1904.

Davis, Henry C. "Negro Folk-Lore in South Carolina." *Journal of American Folk-Lore,* Volume 27, 1914.

Dorson, Richard M. *American Negro Folktales*. Bloomington, Ind.: Indiana University Press, 1958. Reprint, New York: Fawcett Books, A Fawcett Premier Original, 1967.

———. *Negro Tales from Pine Bluff, Arkansas, and Calvin, Michigan*. Folklore Series Number 12. Bloomington, Ind.: Indiana University Press, 1958.

Dundes, Alan, editor. *Mother Wit from the Laughing Barrel*. Englewood Cliffs, N.J.: Prentice-Hall, Inc., 1973.

Fortier, Alcee D. *Louisiana Folk-Tales*. Published for the American Folk-Lore Society. London: Houghton, Mifflin & Co., 1895. Reprint, Millwood, N.Y.: Kraus Reprint Co., 1976.

Gonzales, Ambrose Elliot. *The Black Border: Gullah Stories of the Carolina Coast (with a Glossary)*. Columbia, S.C.: The State Company, 1922.

Jagendorf, M. A. *Folk Stories of the South*. New York: The Vanguard Press, Inc., 1972.

Newell, William Wells. *The Journal of American Folk-Lore*. Published for the American Folk-Lore Society. Boston and New York: Houghton, Mifflin & Co., 1890.

Ohio Oral History Project. Funded by C.E.T.A. and conducted by Tony Dallas, 1979–1980. Yellow Springs, Ohio. Interview copies and audiotapes are available in the Yellow Springs Public Library.

Parsons, Elsie Clews, collector. "Folklore from the Cape Verde Islands." *Memoirs of the American Folk-Lore Society*, Volume 15, Part I, Number 18. Cambridge, Mass.: The Cosmos Press, Inc., 1923.

———. "Folklore of the Sea Islands, South Carolina." *Memoirs of the American Folk-Lore Society*, Volume 26, 1943.

Puckett, Newbell Niles. *Folk Beliefs of the Southern Negro*. Chapel Hill, N.C.: University of North Carolina Press, 1926.

Terrill, Tom E., and Jerrold Hirsch, editors. *Such As Us: Southern Voices of the Thirties*. From the WPA Federal Writers' Project Materials. Chapel Hill, N.C.: University of North Carolina Press, 1978.

ABOUT THE AUTHOR

Virginia Hamilton is one of the most distinguished writers of our time. Winner of the National Book Award, the international Hans Christian Andersen Medal, the Edgar Allan Poe Award, and the Regina Medal, she is the author of *M. C. Higgins the Great,* which was awarded the Newbery Medal and the *Boston Globe–Horn Book* Award, as well as *Sweet Whispers, Brother Rush; The Planet of Junior Brown;* and *In the Beginning,* all Newbery Honor Books. Her books of folklore include *The People Could Fly,* winner of the Coretta Scott King Award; and *Many Thousand Gone: African Americans from Slavery to Freedom.* For The Blue Sky Press, she has written the novel *Plain City,* an ALA Notable Book, and most recently, *Jaguarundi,* a picture book. She has been awarded the 1995 Laura Ingalls Wilder Medal as well as honorary doctorates from both the Bank Street College of Education and the Ohio State University. Ms. Hamilton lives in Ohio with her husband, poet Arnold Adoff.

ABOUT THE ILLUSTRATORS

Leo and Diane Dillon are two of America's most creative and prized illustrators, and together they have illustrated more than twenty-five picture books for children. Awarded the Caldecott Medal twice, for *Ashanti to Zulu* and the West African story *Why Mosquitoes Buzz in People's Ears,* their list of honors includes four *Boston Globe–Horn Book* Awards, two Coretta Scott King Awards, three *New York Times* Best Illustrated Awards, and the Society of Illustrators Gold Medal. Their recent books include Virginia Hamilton's *The People Could Fly* and *Many Thousand Gone: African Americans from Slavery to Freedom;* Nancy Willard's *The Sorcerer's Apprentice* and *Pish, Posh, Said Hieronymus Bosch;* and most recently, *What Am I?,* a concept book for young children. The Dillons are currently the United States' nominees for the 1996 Hans Christian Andersen Medal, and they have been awarded honorary doctorates from Parsons School of Design. They live in New York City.

The pictures in this book were painted with acrylics on illustration board.
The book was printed on eighty-pound Nymolla Matte paper.
The text type was set in Symbol Medium by Monotype Composition
Company, Inc., Baltimore, Maryland.
The display type was set in Copperplate Gothic and Liberty.
Color separations were made by Bright Arts, Ltd., Singapore.
Printed and bound by Tien Wah Press, Singapore.
Production Supervision by Angela Biola
Designed by Kathleen Westray